Alcohol Ink Painting For Complete Beginners

Hattie .I Michael

All rights reserved. Copyright © 2023 Hattie .I Michael

COPYRIGHT © 2023 Hattie .I Michael

All rights reserved.

I listen to a lot of TED talks and motivational speakers. - Jordan Burroughs

Do not weep; do not wax indignant. Understand. - Baruch Spinoza

One may miss the mark by aiming too high as too low. - Thomas Fuller

I started doing motivational tours. I've seen all kinds of people, from the CEOs to the lowest executive, opening up to their fears. We don't introspect as much as we should. - Anupam Kher

Introduction

Welcome to the captivating world of alcohol ink painting, where vibrant colors blend and flow to create mesmerizing works of art. Whether you're a seasoned artist or a beginner, this book will serve as your guide to exploring the endless possibilities of alcohol ink and unleashing your creativity.

In the first chapter, we will delve into the essence of ink art technique, discovering its unique characteristics and the beauty it brings to your artwork. You'll learn how alcohol ink behaves on different surfaces, creating stunning effects that are sure to captivate your audience.

To embark on your alcohol ink journey, it's essential to familiarize yourself with the materials and tools required for this medium. We will explore the various types of alcohol ink, surfaces to work on, and the importance of selecting the right tools. Additionally, we'll discuss safety precautions to ensure a secure and enjoyable creative process.

Creating a conducive workspace is crucial for a seamless painting experience. We will guide you through the process of preparing your workplace, from organizing your materials to ensuring proper ventilation. These considerations will help you establish an environment that fosters creativity and allows you to fully immerse yourself in your art.

Understanding the different types of hairdryers and their effects on alcohol ink is essential for achieving desired results. We will explore the various hairdryer options and techniques for manipulating the ink's movement and flow on your chosen surface.

Ink types play a significant role in the outcome of your artwork. We will delve into the characteristics of different inks, including metallics, and explore how they can add depth and dimension to your creations. You'll discover the versatility of alcohol inks and the magic they bring to your artwork.

The principles of color and color mixing are fundamental in alcohol ink painting. We will delve into the meaning of colors and how they evoke emotions, as well as explore techniques for creating harmonious color palettes. Understanding color theory will enable you to express yourself effectively and create visually captivating compositions.

Sketching is an integral part of the creative process. We will discuss the importance of sketches and how they serve as a foundation for your alcohol ink paintings. You'll learn techniques for creating sketches and utilizing coloring books or sketchbooks to bring your ideas to life.

Protecting your alcohol ink paintings is crucial for preserving their vibrancy and longevity. We will explore different varnishes and their application methods to ensure the longevity of your artwork. Additionally, we will discuss condensate and its role in enhancing the texture and visual appeal of your paintings.

With the groundwork laid, we will dive into the work process itself, exploring hand positioning and techniques for working with alcohol ink. You'll learn how to manipulate the ink, create textures, and achieve different effects to bring your artistic vision to fruition.

As your skills develop, you'll gain confidence in designing and visualizing your paintings. We will explore techniques for planning compositions, balancing elements, and creating visual impact. This knowledge will empower you to create compelling and visually stunning alcohol ink artworks.

Get ready to unleash your creativity and dive into the captivating world of alcohol ink painting. With this comprehensive guide, you'll develop the skills and techniques needed to create mesmerizing masterpieces that reflect your unique artistic expression. Let the colors flow, and let your imagination soar as you embark on your alcohol ink painting journey.

Contents

1. ABOUT INK ART TECHNIQUE 1
2. MATERIALS AND TOOLS FOR INK ART 2
3. SAFETY WHEN WORKING WITH ALCOHOL INK 5
4. PREPARING THE WORKPLACE 7
5. HAIRDRYER. TYPES 9
6. INK TYPES 12
7. METALLICS 19
8. ALCOHOL, THINNER 23
9. SURFACES TO WORK ON 26
10. COMPOSITION IN ABSTRACT WORKS 31
11. PRINCIPLES OF COLOR. MIXING COLORS. THE MEANING OF COLOR 40
12. CREATING SKETCHES 54
13. COLORING BOOK. SKETCHBOOK 55
14. PROTECTION OF PAINTINGS. VARNISHES 58
15. CONDENSAT 64
16. WORK PROCESS. HAND POSITIONING 65
17. TECHNIQUES FOR WORKING WITH ALCOHOL INK 72

Lesson 1: Practical part. Getting to know the technique of drawing with alcohol ink ... 72
Lesson 2: Monochrome Technique 78
Lesson 3: Drawing on Canvas 81
Lesson 4: The technique of drawing "on the plum. Fleur." 85
Lesson 5: Free Drying Techniques with a Hairdryer 89
Lesson 6: Marble backgrounds and stain effect. Splash effect 91
Lesson 7. Gradients. Drawing in three or more colors 98

Lesson 8: The "edge" or "plissé" technique 103
Lesson 9: Drawing Flowers with theCompressor 108
Lesson 10: The "Rose Handle " technique. 115
Lesson 11: Creating Rings in Ink 121
Lesson 13: Plot works 132
Lesson 14: Applying Alcohol Painting with thePebeo Contour 144
Lesson 15: Decorating paintings withadditional tools and materials 148
Lesson 16: Géode with a brush 154
Lesson 18: The fancy snake technique 162
Lesson 19: Clocks with alcohol ink 166
Lesson 20: Petry 172
Lesson 21: Masking Fluid and ClearSilhouette 178
Lesson 22: Drawing on Glass and Ceramicswith Ink 183
Lesson 23: Black Surfaces 191
Lesson 24: Collages (mini-pictures) 194
18. THE APPLICATION OF PAINTING WITHALCOHOL INK 200
19. DESIGN AND VIZUALIZATION OFPAINTINGS 207

1. ABOUT INK ART TECHNIQUE

The INK ART technique is all about painting with alcohol ink. This technique allows you to create airy, abstract interior paintings without special drawing skills. The colors are alcohol-based inks. Bright, stable ink is a pleasure to watch while interacting with alcohol.

If you pour a little alcohol and add a drop of ink in the center of this puddle, you will see something fascinating.

Before becoming a liquid technique, alcohol ink was used in backgrounds and scrapbooking album decorations. The ink was also used in the printing industry to print vinyl signs.

Alcohol ink paintings quickly gained popularity, thanks to social media in America and Australia. Over time, artists and designers turned their attention to alcohol ink. Today the Ink Art technique is famous all over the world.

The world of alcohol ink is a bright, exciting wonderland where you can bring your wildest ideas to life!

2. MATERIALS AND TOOLS FOR INK ART

The materials are chosen for the specific task based on personal preferences.
Executing decorative painting with alcoholic inks will require materials and tools. Here is a brief list of them.

a) Alcohol-based ink.
b) Isopropylated Absolute Alcohol 99.9%.
c) Basics for drawing:
 -plastic paper (white, black, transparent). Transparent paper is needed for pictures -transformers,
 -Yupo paper (thin absorbent paper),
 -synthetic paper 250, 300, 450 microns (dense non-absorbent paper),
 -tablets with a laminated surface,
 -artboards are tablets with a smooth surface of different shapes,
 -glass,
 -ceramics (tiles, dishes),
 -primed canvases.
d) Hairdryer.
The hairdryer is the brush with which we paint our air paintings.
e) Airbrush. Compressor.
Use to create different effects and interesting floral motifs.
f) Thick film to protect the work surface.
g) Brush with a silicone tip. It's a rescue wand that:
 - It helps guide the flow of alcohol ink where accuracy is essential.
 - Helps mix inks together on paper, especially heavy pigments (gold, silver).
 - Helps to draw lines and connect the edges in the picture.
h) Plastic pipettes. We use them to dilute the ink with alcohol in cups.

i) Transparent bottle with a sharpened alcohol spout. The spout can be either plastic or needle. The needle nose can scratch the surface by pouring alcohol on it, be careful!
j) Spray bottle. Use it for a splashing effect.
k) Paper wipes. These are needed to get rid of excess ink.

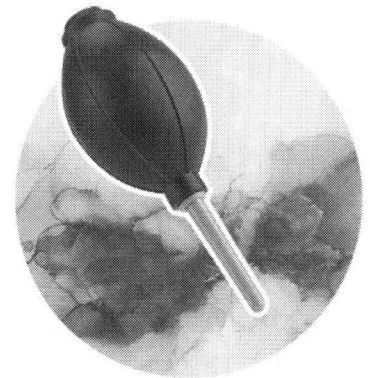

l) Rubber Blower. A handy hand tool for controlling the flow of alcohol ink with air. Use to control air flow by adjusting the pressure when drawing with ink.
m) Plastic or glass cups for diluting ink.
n) Ear sticks. Use to create additional effects in work.
o) Polyethylene film or disposable diapers for pets. Purchased from drugstores. Use to protect the workplace.
p) Pebeo Masking Fluid. Used to create additional effects.

q) Water brash. A water brush with a reservoir that you fill with isopropyl alcohol. Used to create effects in paintings.

❖ Adjusting the flow of alcohol is simple - squeeze the reservoir, and the flow of alcohol will increase.
❖ You can wash the brush hairs with alcohol (iso).

r) UV protective varnish for works and fixing varnish.
s) Epoxy resin. Apply for a glossy finish (optional).
t) Princeton Catalyst Tools. A silicone tool moves alcohol ink and acrylic paints on surfaces.

3. SAFETY WHEN WORKING WITH ALCOHOL INK

Observe safety precautions when working with the technique of drawing with alcohol ink.

1. We work in a ventilated room.
2. Protect the respiratory system with a respirator. A typical construction or semi-professional respirator is suitable.

❖ *Professional protection is recommended when working with large amounts of isopropyl alcohol and drawing with alcohol ink for a long time (3M mask - respirator with interchangeable filters FFP3). A 3M full-face mask is used for mucous membrane problems. Filters should be changed as the mask is used. If you experience difficulty or smell breathing in the mask, it is time to replace the filters.*

3. Protect your hands with nitrile or vinyl gloves.

❖ Highly pigmented alcohol ink can eat into the skin on your hands and is very difficult to wash off. It dries the skin on your hands.

4. The apron protects your clothes, which can get ink on them.

❖ The ink is practically impossible to wash off. If you find an ink remedy, please email me at info@artan-studio.com
❖ Isopropyl alcohol does not accumulate in the human body as it does with epoxy resin. If large amounts of isopropyl alcohol are used, minor vapor poisoning may occur. Be careful!
❖ Clean soiled hands or table with isopropyl alcohol. After working with alcohol, wash your hands with soap and water and apply the cream.
❖ Alcohol ink is not recommended for young children under 14 years of age, pregnant women, asthmatics, and people who are sensitive to the smell of alcohol.
There may be slight poisoning from large amounts of isopropyl alcohol vapor.

4. PREPARING THE WORKPLACE

Decorative painting with alcohol ink will require great care in preparing your work surface before starting. The workspace must be spacious for your work.

1. Protect the work surface with plastic film. The thick film can be used many times.

❖ *You can use disposable medical diapers or pet diapers. They are available at drugstores. Any excess ink that runs off will be absorbed into the diaper.*

2. The work surface must be level and without a slope. Check the work surface with a building level or the "Level" app on your phone.

❖ *If the surface is uneven, your drawing using one of the self-drying techniques will shift to the side, and the whole idea will float away with the ink.*

3. While working with alcohol ink, ventilate the room nicely.
4. Prepare vinyl/nitrile gloves for work.
5. Prepare a 3M respirator with charcoal filters.

6. Use a protective apron or creative clothing against accidental ink spills.
7. Apply dry wipes. There should be enough of them.
8. Have a box/bucket for used ink wipes.
9. Have plastic or glass cups for alcohol.
10. We use pipettes to work with the ink.
11. Prepare the hair dryer.
12. Alcohol ink.
13. Itten's color wheel.

❖ *Clean soiled hands or a table quickly with alcohol before the ink is absorbed.*

5. HAIRDRYER. TYPES

We get air paintings in this technique with the help of a hairdryer. But what is the suitable hairdryer to use in drawing with ink?

1. Choose a **travel hairdryer** with small power ranging **from 600 W to 1200 W** with temperature mode switches.

The temperature mode of a road hairdryer can be either hot airflow or cold airflow. There is not much difference between the two. They will both do the job. Precise edges are more difficult to make with a road blow dryer than with other dryers.

2. The second type of hairdryer is a **hairdryer-comb** with a small output **of 400 W to 1000 W** with temperature mode switches. There is a narrow and wide nozzle. The wide nozzle hairdryer is better than the one with a narrow nozzle because it gets more work done. When using a hairdryer-comb, you get a beautiful edge due to the hot airflow speed. With this hair

dryer, you can work on any surface. There is slight warping of paper when working with a hairdryer (if it is less than 200 microns), but it quickly evens out when it cools down.

3. You can use **a hairdryer for embossing.** With it, we achieve many edges due to the flow of hot air that comes out of it faster and dries the alcohol.

Work on complex, non-absorbable surfaces (art-boards) with an embossing hairdryer. Such a hairdryer can melt the paper and deform the surface. This hair dryer is more often used for scrapbooking. Buy it in the art stores.

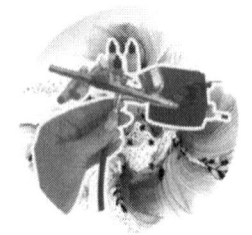

4. Airbrush. Compressor.

An airbrush is a brush with which we spray paint under pressure. We don't pour paint inside the airbrush, instead, we press the trigger of the airbrush and paint with a stream of air by tilting its handle.

We work with a cold air stream in the airbrush compressor, moving the ink in the right direction. Working time with the airbrush increases due to the cold stream. As a result, unusual and beautiful paintings are created.

The airbrush is used to create different effects and interesting floral motifs.

❖   *It is not recommended to **use a construction** hair dryer to draw on synthetic paper because of its power. With high power, you will not be able to form the desired drawing. The paper will deform, and your ink will absorb quickly.*

6. INK TYPES

There are a massive number of alcohol-based inks on the market. But the quality of these inks varies. When choosing a cheap material, understand that it may not be durable. An essential characteristic of ink is lightfastness.

Here is a list of alcohol inks and their properties:

1. **There are low-concentration and concentrated inks**.

These are alcohol inks and refills by Ranger /Adirondack /Tim Holtz, Huids, Touch, Media Ink/Pentart.

- Ranger /Adirondack /Tim Holtz.

They are liquid, low-pigment ink. The ink consumption will be higher than that of other companies. These inks produce weightless, airy compositions. Shades range from saturated to semi-transparent.

Solvent: isopropyl alcohol.

The range of colors: 48 colors and shades, white (Mixative), and four metallics - gold, silver, mother of pearl, and copper.

When the ink dries, it sometimes gives an entirely different shade to the paper. The ink loses color and turns a pink hue when you mix purple with white. There have been cases where the purple color

(Purple Twilight) burned out entirely over time.
Volume: 15 ml, 60 ml.
Country of Origin: America

- Huids.
This company's inks are very expressive and bright.
Color palette: 23 transparent colors and 14 opaque colors. The opaque colors are specially designed for use on dark surfaces.

Metallic gold is superb!!!

Volume: 30 ml
Country of origin: Germany.

- Touch, Refill ink.
This ink has an exciting color palette.

Color gamut: 46 colors and shades. The colors hold up well. The lighter shades of this ink curl. There is more oiliness in them.

Volume: 20 ml
Country of origin: South Korea.

- Media ink/Pentart.
An acid-free ink with beautiful dark shades.

The ink has a strong odor. It is oily. It is compatible with acrylic paints. When working with these inks, we use isopropyl alcohol or thinner only. With ethyl alcohol, such pigments (ink) can curdle.

Volume: 20 ml
Country of origin: Hungary.

2. Highly concentrated inks.

These include refills by Copic, Piñata, and silver by Molotow Liquid chrome.

- COPIC.

This ink has a glossy effect after drying. Such inks are bright, have transparent colors, and do not produce a residue. Their earthy and blue shades are highly concentrated. They do not have bright visible oily borders from the ink. Great for air voiles.

Color gamut: 350 colors and shades.

Features: Refills allow for individual color mixing. May precipitate when mixed with other inks.

Volume: 12 ml for the new line, 25 ml for the old line.

Country of Origin: Japan

- Piñata Jacquard.

These inks have a dense, concentrated, and saturated color palette. There may be oily borders around the edge of the ink. The high pigment concentration allows such inks to produce vivid and more profound colors.

The ink does not lose color when mixing purple with white. It remains purple.

Solvent: denatured alcohol (a type of ethyl alcohol).

Color range: 18 colors; 4 metallic colors - gold, silver, pearl, bronze, brass, and pure white - matte, opaque.

The white color is ideal for dark surfaces and the petri technique.

Volume: 15 ml, 29 ml

Country of Origin: America

- Silver by Molotow Liquid chrome.

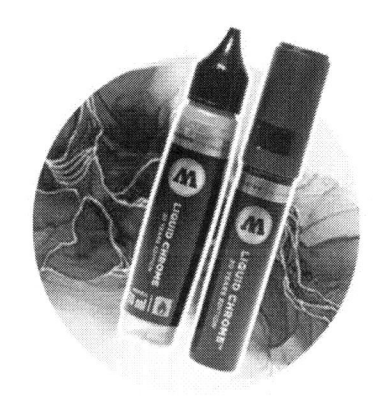

These are highly pigmented special marker inks. They are unique in their mirror effect, scratch and erase resistance. They have good resistance to UV radiation. This ink creates an actual mirror effect. It can be sprayed from a compressor. There are also markers and felt-tip pens for additional effects.

Volume: 30 ml
Country of Origin: Germany

3. **The delaminating ink**.

Only the Russian brand "Kamenskaya" is familiar with such ink properties. These inks give off residue. If you choose an exciting pattern texture, it can look exciting.

Color scheme: 25 colors
Volume: 15 ml
Country of Origin: Russia.

❖ *We dilute the highly concentrated ink with alcohol (iso) and get the tone.*

As I do. Example:

I pour isopropyl alcohol (3-4 full droppers) into a glass or plastic beaker and add 1-2 drops of highly concentrated ink. I shake the alcohol with the ink, apply the ink with a pipette to the surface and start blowing with a hairdryer.

Ink storage.

Screw in your ink tightly. The ink may evaporate because it contains alcohol.

Avoid direct sunlight. An ink storage organizer for petite and tall bottles is available on Amazon.

To make these organizers yourself, all you need is a plastic container and foam rubber. Make round notches in the foam rubber according to your diameter for the ink.

❖ *I recommend that beginners start with Pinata ink. With Pinata, you get beautiful, vibrant drawings.*

❖ *We make coloring sheets of all the inks and sign them. This is very handy for painting, for finding the right color (see "Coloring. Sketchbook").*

❖ *Shake the ink before opening it. Do not open the ink over the surface where you will draw. Tiny ink particles can get on your work and be hard to remove.*

❖ *Inks from different manufacturers mix well with each other.*

7. METALLICS

Paintings with alcohol ink are unusual and exciting, but if you add metallic hues (gold, silver, bronze), they give the paintings even more sparkle.

There are many metallic inks on the market. These are quick-drying, alcohol-based dyes.

Using alcohol, metallics lay down in beautiful spots, lines, and islands, forming metallic shimmers. If you use metallic inks without alcohol or thinner, the dyes will be as a dense layer on the surface, forming a solid metallic surface.

We add metallics either at once with the ink and alcohol at the beginning of the work or on a surface that has not finished drying and then dry it with a hairdryer.

After the ink is done, use a fine brush to finish your painting with metallics. Add 1-2 drops of undiluted metallics on the palette and use the brush to create a pattern on the painting. Don't forget to shake.

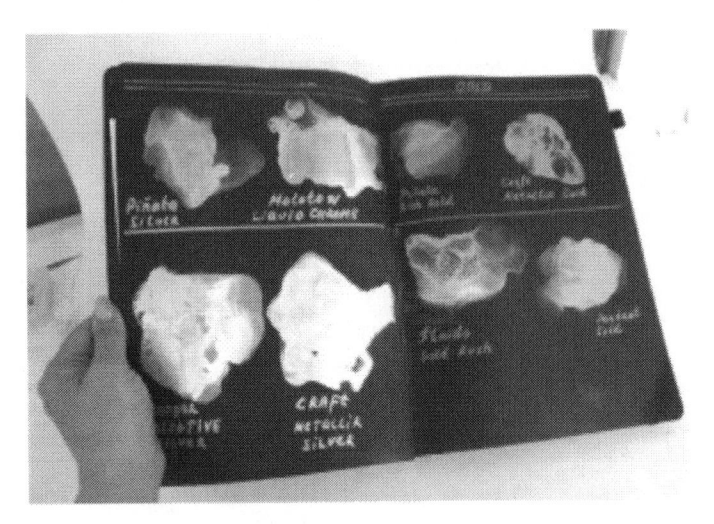

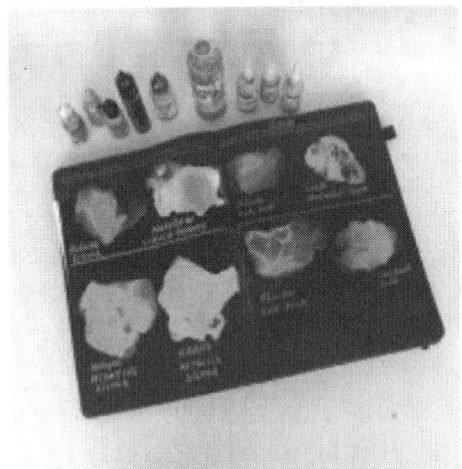

Metallic dyes from different manufacturers do not have the same shade.
And finding exactly your shade will help you find the metallic ink dyes.

My observations:

-Pinata "Brass Gold." Ink - it lays down beautifully, brightly, and evenly. The gold does not mix with the color.

-Piñata "Gold" ink - the color goes "green." The ink loses its covering power.

-Pentart "Gold" ink is very oily, "dirty", and translucent.

-The best gold is Huids ink. The gold is so bright that you can mistake it for gilding when it dries. They are very opaque and don't mix with the color.

- The best silver ink from Molotow Liquid chrome. This highly pigmented ink is also used for markers. Its mirrored surface will dazzle, and you can see yourself in the reflection.)

❖   *Shake any metallics before working.*

- *Metallic color settles; it is heavier than ordinary ink and reveals the color with a brush or finger.*
- *It is diluted with metallic alcohol, so it goes oily (it will not be a solid stain).*

8. ALCOHOL, THINNER

Alcohol is used for diluting ink, brightening, blending, and removing color in works of this technique.
The different types of alcohols used in drawing with alcohol ink are:

- Isopropyl alcohol.
Isopropyl alcohol, 99.9% absolute. The alcohol concentration should preferably be at least 96%.
Isopropanol increases the drying time of alcohol ink, slowly spreading the ink over the synthetic paper, producing beautifully crisp edges in the works.
Pros: reasonable price and volumes. We buy such alcohol in construction stores.
The disadvantage of isopropyl alcohol is that it has a strong odor and is toxic. After working with isopropanol, paintings should be secured with a protective varnish.

- Alcohol-based solvents with additives.
Few companies on the market offer such solutions.
For example, Ranger Adirondack Alcohol Blending Solution.
Blending is low-toxic, fast-drying alcohol that serves as a diluent with the ink. It fixes the ink by forming a film - a protective surface. After working with blending, we cover the work with a fixing varnish.
Pros: weak odor.
Cons: significantly more expensive than isopropyl alcohol. Not available in all art stores, on Amazon.

- Ethanol alcohol 96.6% (ethanol, medical alcohol).

With ethanol alcohol, we do not get faces, but we get exciting effects and the texture of the pattern. The effects are grainy and blurred due to the rapid evaporation of alcohol. Iso-propanol, on the other hand, evaporates at a constant rate. It all depends on the artist's request.

If the ink quality is low and ethanol has evaporated, some water drops can remain in the picture. Such drops are also called worm drops.

Pros - has minimal odor.

Please remember to observe safety precautions with alcohol!

- In a well-ventilated room, the alcohol will not harm your body.

- Alcohol vapor, which evaporates and rises upward, escapes with a fresh air intake. However, mild intoxication and nausea may occur if the room is closed and poorly ventilated.

- Ink is easily flammable, so I recommend keeping the bottles away from fire.

- Alcohol should not be taken internally!

- We use a 3M protective mask. For small volumes, you can use a small 3M mask; for large volumes of alcohol, you can use a mask.

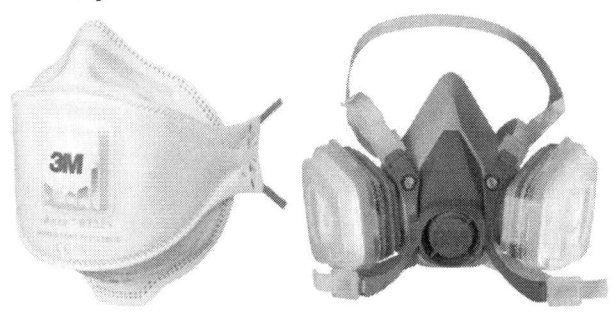

❖ The quality of the alcohol affects the quality of the drawing. For example, alcohol that is less than 96%, exhausted, or has become more watery gives a residue or dripping effect. When the alcohol is not watery, it forms an even, beautiful surface.
❖ If the humidity is high! The picture will not get a nice edge, or there will be a dripping effect.
❖ Alcohol at lower concentrations will not work. Alcohol ink can curdle, precipitate, and have a "torn edge" effect.
❖ Isopropanol lasts longer than blending. Isopropanol gives the ink a better flow, so you get artistic patterns.
❖ Close the bottle with the alcohol tightly when working. Don't forget that alcohol evaporates very quickly.
❖ All solvents and alcohols can be mixed.
❖ Keep the alcohol in a dark place.

9. SURFACES TO WORK ON

What do you draw on with alcohol ink? This technique requires non-porous, non-absorbent surfaces. Alcohol ink works best on a smooth surface.

Other surfaces we can use include:

1) **Plastic paper** (white, black, transparent).

The plastic sheet is polyethylene with good density—an excellent material for drawing with alcohol ink. Black plastic has a porous and matte surface. It is slightly more difficult to spread ink on it than on white. It is harder to erase ink from such a surface. The paper is not deformed.

We use a transparent plastic sheet to create transformer paintings.

2) **Synthetic paper**: 250, 300, 350, 450, 515 microns.

It is a synthetic material based on polypropylene, which does not absorb moisture, and has a smooth surface. The greater the density of paper, the better!

This technique is the most common option for drawing. The properties of plastic film are elasticity and durability.

Such paper is reusable and dense. With the help of alcohol, it is easy to erase the unnecessary element in the picture and draw again.

Synthetic paper is suitable for spreading alcohol ink. It is scratch-resistant.

Blue, Purple, and Magenta are the ink colors that leave a slight smudge when rubbed out with alcohol. We can completely erase the alcohol ink from surfaces with a melamine sponge.

❖ Apply rubbing alcohol to the spot where the ink is worse, leave for 2 minutes, and use a melamine sponge to remove the stain.
❖ Recommendation - don't leave such dark colors on the paper for too long if you want to reuse it.
❖ Frame the synthetic paper or glue it to a wooden surface.

3) **Yupo paper** is a synthetic polypropylene-based material that does not absorb moisture and has a smooth surface. It is scratch-resistant, absorbs ink quickly, and cannot be thoroughly washed away with alcohol. The paper can only be used once.

4) **Tablets with a laminated surface**.
These are any smooth wooden surfaces - MDF, PVC. The substrate of such tablets is usually dense. The tablet surface does

not bend when primed with epoxy resin.
A primer is required for these surfaces.

5) **Artboards**.
Artboard is framed or poured with epoxy resin. It is made of MDF with a unique laminated coating, not porous, creating a perfectly smooth surface. No primer is required for these boards.

6) **Photo paper**.
We use glossy photo paper (Canon Photo Paper Pro Platinum 300 **g/m²**; Inkjet - Papier Unicorn).

7) **Artboards with a metal coating.** These boards are usually made with an aluminum baguette. On this board, the picture looks very unusual.

8) **Glass, plexiglass**.
With the help of a transparent surface, we get exciting effects that we can frame.

9) **White ceramics (tiles, ceramic tableware).** When we coat the finished work with a protective varnish, the ink on it will be protected from external exposure—an exciting option for small works.

10) **Canvas**. The canvas should be well stretched without sagging, and with wedges to increase tension.

For example, a fine-grain linen canvas with a high stretcher is a good option. This canvas is usually already coated with a primer to keep the ink from soaking in. If the canvas sags, the ink will flow to the center.

Smaller canvases can be hung on the wall at once, and more significant works can have an additional rope for hanging.

The ink on the canvas is immediately secured with a protective varnish (matte) or covered with epoxy resin - the choice is yours.

In my book "the resin guide", you will learn how to properly coat canvases with epoxy. The link is below.
https://amzn.to/3xLI04I

11) **Plastic** is another surface to work with ink.

12) **Epoxy resin**.

Such pictures with ink are made in layers - first, we apply ink, then transparent resin, ink again, and then epoxy resin. That's how we get a 3D painting.

10. COMPOSITION IN ABSTRACT WORKS

Drawing begins with the compositional arrangement of images on the canvas. How the image is composed will largely determine the overall impression of the painting.

For your painting to attract attention, you need to understand the drawing composition. Learn to look at paintings with compositional diagrams to understand the author's techniques better.

Composition diagrams are imaginary lines in which the elements of a work are organized. Paintings painted in spirit ink mostly have a non-figurative composition. This format is very close to abstractionism.

Abstract (formal) composition is the absence of a theme. Here we do not see the apparent meaning, but we feel the author's mood by the colors, shape, and texture of the canvas on which we build the composition.

Such pictures lose the bottom and the top; they are viewed and turned from either side, and they do not reflect reality.

Use the ink to create color harmony in your work. The peculiarity of ink is similar to watercolor, with airy shapes and blurs. Our task is not just to pour the ink on the surface (although you can do that too) but to follow some rules or **principles of composition.**

One of the basic principles of composition is **three-component** - when we use three sizes of an object, three different directions, and three different tones to ensure the picture is harmonious.

When there are no objects in our works, the composition is subject to **the three features of composition:**

1. Dominant - a pronounced compositional center - is where the viewer's attention is concentrated. As a rule, this will be the most contrasting place in your picture. We use color (alcohol ink) to highlight the compositional center.

The point of intersection of the composition is called **the geometric center of the composition.**
If you place a spot of color in this center, it will look harmonious. To give our pictures dynamics, you can shift the compositional center. To create a sense of lightness in the composition, it is better to apply a contrasting stain just above the geometric center of the sheet. The format of the sheet is vertical.

2. Equilibrium is a state where everything is balanced relative to the compositional center. So is the placement of the elements of the composition in which the visual association with the weight of all the elements (color spots) creates the impression of stability. No one side of the work should not outweigh such a composition.

Our eyes perceive the image better by moving from left to right than from right to left. To achieve balance in the composition, shift the image to the right.

3. Integrity is the stage of completeness of a composition, where no part of the whole can be removed, moved, or added to. The main thing is to have a sense of integrity and balance in the color patches in your work.

Without composition, paintings would have no visual logic or meaning.

Compositions are:

- **Closed** - when the elements (spots of color) do not go beyond the borders (the picture). The gaze moves from any place in the composition to its center.

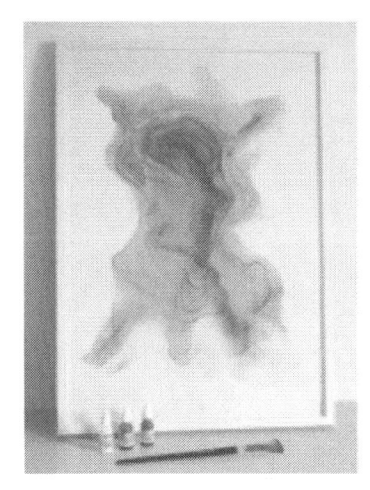

- **Open** - when the spots of color tend to be outside the borders (the picture frame).

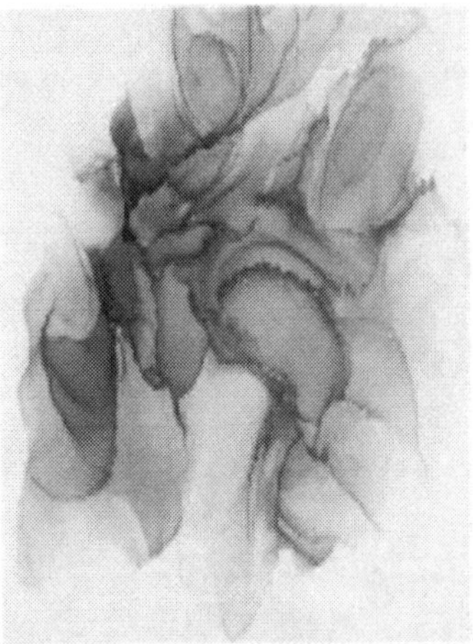

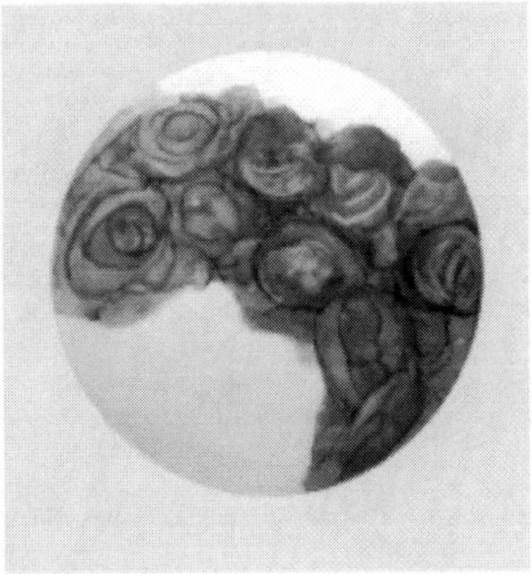

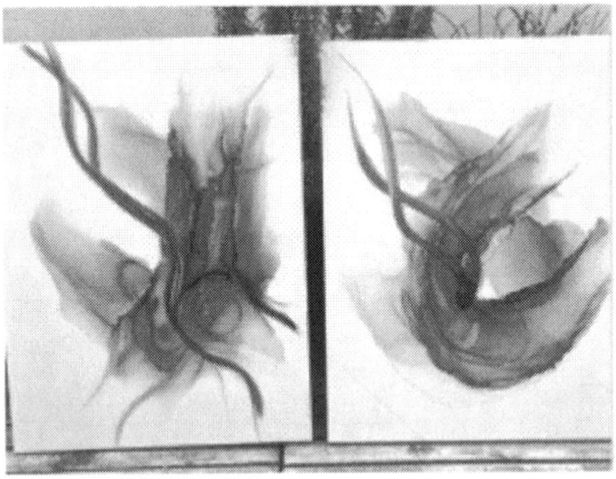

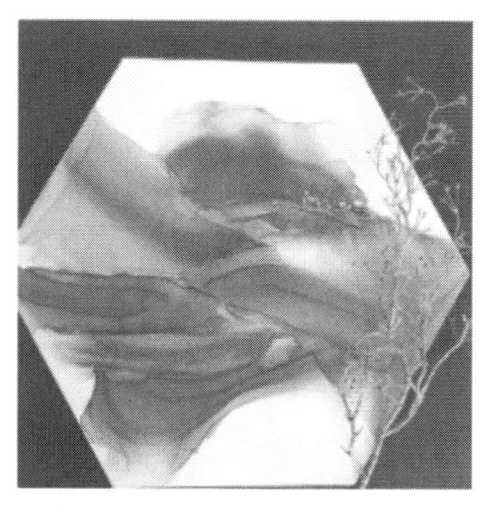

The rules of rhythm are the regular alternation and repetition of elements. When repetitive elements, patterns, dots, or spots of color are set throughout the work, your painting will look calm and flowing.

This is how the human eye focuses on the central part of the painting.

With the help of **the rules of composition,** we achieve harmony in the works.

I will write briefly about the main rules of composition applied in creating abstract paintings.

Fibonacci number. The golden ratio rule or the proportion of divine harmony. When the proportions of an image reflect the proportions of the golden ratio, imagine an invisible spiral and create a drawing.

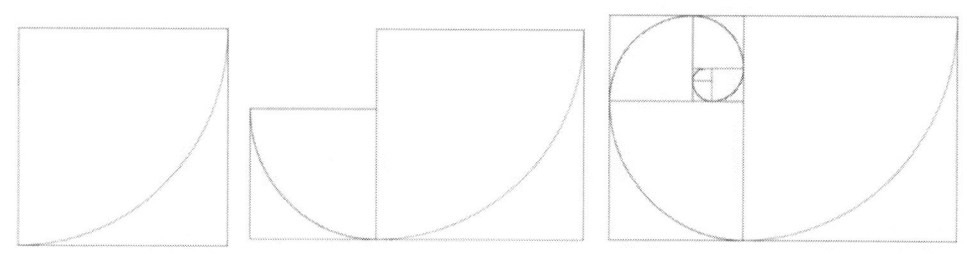

The rule of thirds is a simplified version of the golden ratio, dividing a composition into thirds.

How do you apply it to your work?

Visually divide the picture into nine equal squares. At the intersection of these squares will be focal points (points of intersection). It has been observed that a person always concentrates on these points. If objects (spots of color) are located along the third line, the composition looks more harmonious.

Place the compositional center in the central rectangle to achieve a harmonious composition.

When creating work in spirit ink, the arrangement of the main color spots goes on the focal points. There will be the main center (a darker ink spot) and the secondary compositional center.

❖ *It is not necessary to use all four points in most cases!*

When making use of three focal points, use the diagonal principle of dynamic composition to convey mood. The diagonal line helps to convey movement. This line is directed diagonally, and the drawing goes upward (example below).

The rhythm of the diagonal directions gives activity to the composition. Diagonal principles are good for abstraction.

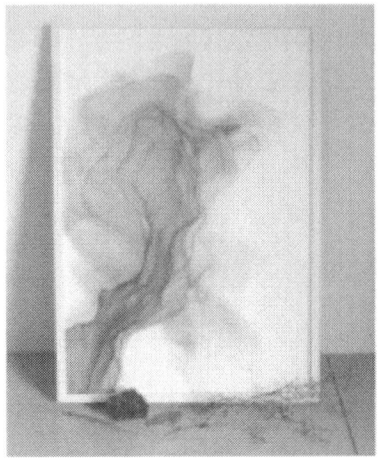

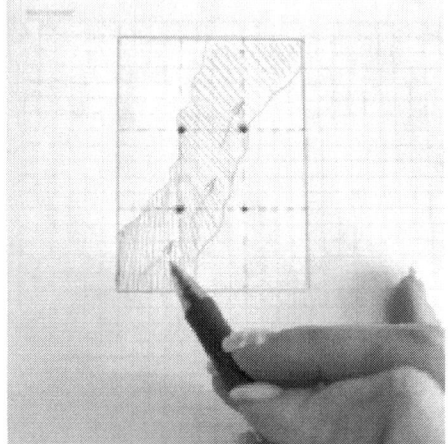

Lines can be diagonal, curved, spiral, or crossed.

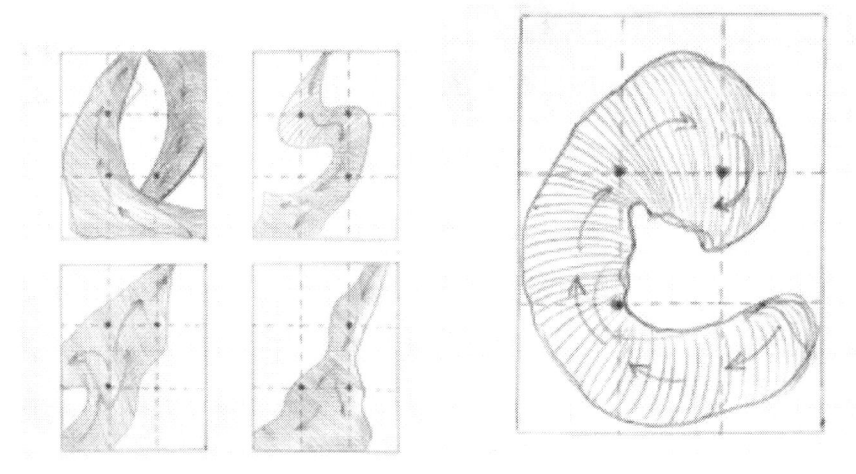

A few examples of revealing a sense of dynamics:

Static composition - the center of gravity of the entire composition should be within the support area of this composition.

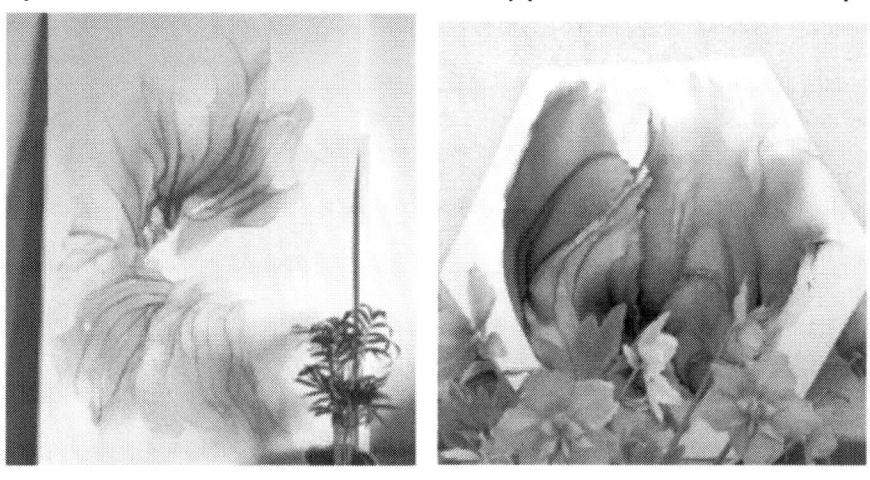

Since we perceive paintings from left to the right, we use this nuance for harmony.

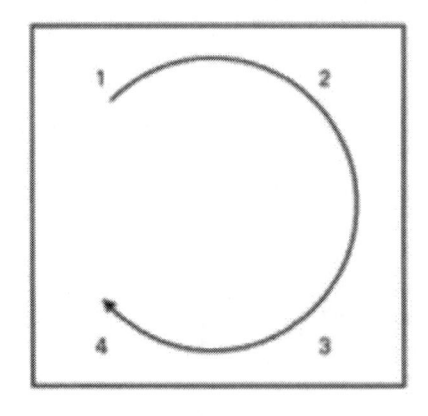

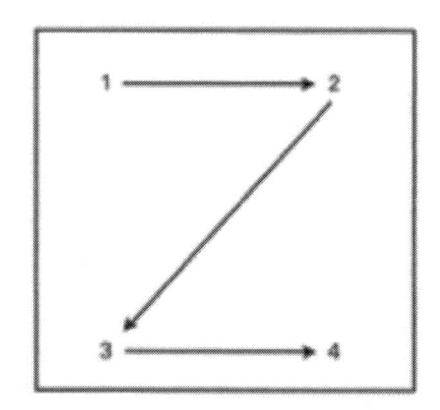

There is the principle of symmetry, where all the placement of color spots are symmetrically arranged on the canvas, and everything is balanced. In a symmetrical composition, all the pieces are balanced, that is, balanced in mass, tone, color, and in terms of the spaces between them. This is a simple type of composition that gives a static result.

In asymmetric composition, there is no balance if the semantic center is closer to the edge of the picture.

In my abstract paintings, I avoid symmetry. I mentally make touchpoints asymmetrical to make the work more dynamic and exciting. If the lines are clearly in the center, the picture will be uninteresting.

A person's visual perception of the spots of color in a picture:
- Bright spots of color look heavier than muted ones;
- The color spot on the right has more weight than the spot on the left;
- Any spot of color at the top of the picture looks heavier than the spot at the bottom;
- Vertically placed forms seem heavier than slanted forms;
- The area of dark space should be more prominent in the picture than the white space;

- Preferably the darker shades are placed in the center and the lighter shades on the edges;

Do not think through the picture beforehand because abstraction is about feelings and states. Mix and distribute the ink on the surface as you wish. Your emotions and imagination will be reflected in the paintings.

To make pictures look harmonious, not just one messy spot, learn the basics of color science in the next section.

- ❖ *Dark fills visually shrink the picture, and light fills vice versa.*
- ❖ *The round format of the tablet will give your picture a calm finish.*
- ❖ *The rectangular format of the painting increases the vast impression of the image so the picture won't turn out too saturated, too dark, or leave more air, i.e., white.*

11. PRINCIPLES OF COLOR. MIXING COLORS. THE MEANING OF COLOR

"Human emotion can only be conveyed in color, without resorting to the depiction of real objects" /Kandinsky/.

Color is essential to the artist because the correct application of color is one of the conditions for a successful drawing. With the correct use of this or that color, it is possible to convey a mood or evoke an emotional state in the viewer. A high degree of memorization is predetermined by the presence of stable associations associated with a particular color.

Everyone knows there are seven base colors in nature, but there are only three tones (blue, yellow, and red) for the human eye. We get an ample palette of colors by adding white to each tone. White acts as an additional color.

When mixing these three base colors, we get secondary colors or colors of the second group.

For example, we get orange, blue, and red-violet (colors of the second group) by mixing red and yellow.

We get six more colors from the third group by mixing each color with the neighboring color.

All colors are divided into **chromatic colors** (colored, all colors of the rainbow) and **achromatic** colors (neutral, colorless - the whole gradation from black to white).

Achromatic colors are combined with all chromatic colors, as all these colors (black, white, and gray) are not colors. Color harmony is all shades of **chromatic** colors.

All colors are divided into warm and cool colors. Warm colors fill the interior with coziness, lift your spirits, and cause positive emotions. Cold colors fill the space with freshness and energy. This palette is suitable for active, creative people.

The basic principles of color that you need to know and understand. The three properties of color are:
1. Hue is the name of the colors (e.g., red, yellow, blue).
2. Saturation is the whiteness or darkness of a hue (color). The purer the color, the more saturated it is.
3. Intensity - determines the brightness and dullness of the hue (color).

To simplify the choice of a harmonious combination of colors, we use **a color circle (Itten's circle).** The author of the color circle is Johannes Itten, a Swiss artist, and theorist.

This is a color combination tool that helps you create color harmony. **Color harmony is a** beautiful balance and unity of colors. It leaves the eye with a feeling of complete balance. The color wheel is an excellent aid in color selection for designers, artists, and other creatives.
In Itten's circle, harmonious color combinations can be placed against each other with the help of geometric shapes (squares, triangles, rectangles). If we look at the Itten circle, we will see a

beautiful harmonious combination of colors at the corners of these figures.

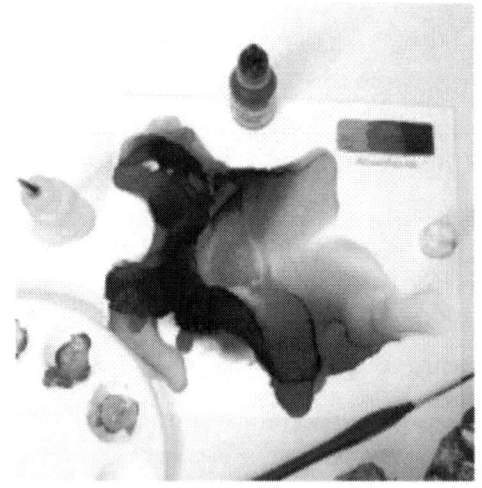

Combination options:

1. **Monochrome harmony is a** combination of the same color in different saturations. Monochromatic colors can be diluted with neutral (achromatic) colors when a single color is used on the color wheel, applying varying degrees of saturation - from dark to light.

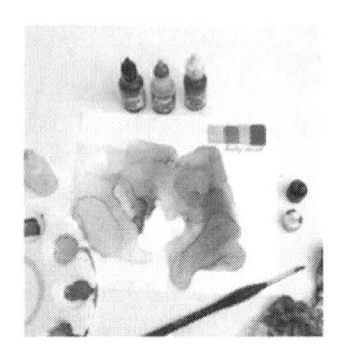

2. **Harmony of related colors (analog triad).** This is when we use neighbor colors on the color wheel.

When we use neighbor colors, such colors change each other.

Red will no longer combine all of the same properties that it carries in isolation. For example, when red and yellow are next to each other in a picture, they are not as actively revealed. There will be no muddying with these colors when the ink is mixed.

❖ ***An essential rule of thumb is** to consider the proportions of your colors. When choosing two colors, don't use equal proportions of the chosen colors. If you use colors in equal proportions, they can overpower each other.*

For example, when using yellow and purple, you will need more purple than yellow (¼ to ¾). One color will need to be the accent color in the picture, and the other will need to be the primary (dominant) color. Use orange and blue (1/3: ¾); red and green = ½)

You can get more information on contrast in color spot areas on your own from books or on the Internet.

3. **Complementary harmony (opposite colors).** The colors are opposite each other in a color circle. This combination of colors mutually enhances each other.
When mixing colors of opposites, the gray color is always the result. (For example: purple and yellow, green and red). Here, those colors that give grey (additional) influence the perception of our eye in the most harmonious way.

4. The color combinations are evenly distributed, forming a classic equilateral triangle **(Classic Triad)**.

These are the colors stacked on the sides of an equilateral triangle.

5. Scheme of the three-color combination on the color circle according to the principle of an acute triangle **(Contrast Triad)**.

6. The color combinations are evenly distributed, forming a square **(Square Harmony)**. All four colors are in harmony with each other.

7. Combination of two pairs of complementary colors, forming a rectangle **(Rectangular Harmony)**

There are also different types of contrasting colors. With the help of these colors, we give expressiveness to the picture.

The first type of contrast is the colors of opposite, complementary colors: (red and green, in life, are red poppies; yellow and purple are pansies). Such work looks consistently winning, more catchy, and bright.

Another type of contrasting color is a combination of warm and cool shades of colors. For example, when using red (warm), add blue (excellent). Such contrasts bring the work to life.

The third type of contrast is the contrast between light and warm. Choose any color (dark, red hue) and add the lightest hue (blue hue). You will also have a contrasting work. In museums and exhibitions, red-blue paintings are the quickest to sell.

By focusing on all these rules and knowing them, you will consciously choose colors and understand what feelings and emotions your viewer will get.

For beginners, I recommend not using more than three colors. Start with a simple monochrome scheme (use one color and its shades). Then apply the classic monochrome scheme - take one light color and add a neutral color (from gray to black shades). Then connect the complementary gamut and try to work with three or more colors.

The correct ratio of color spots in the picture:

60% is the primary color, which will be the dominant color.

30% is the contrast color, which supports the visual interest of the viewer.

10% is the accent color.

Below is a color scheme for the harmonious combination of colors.

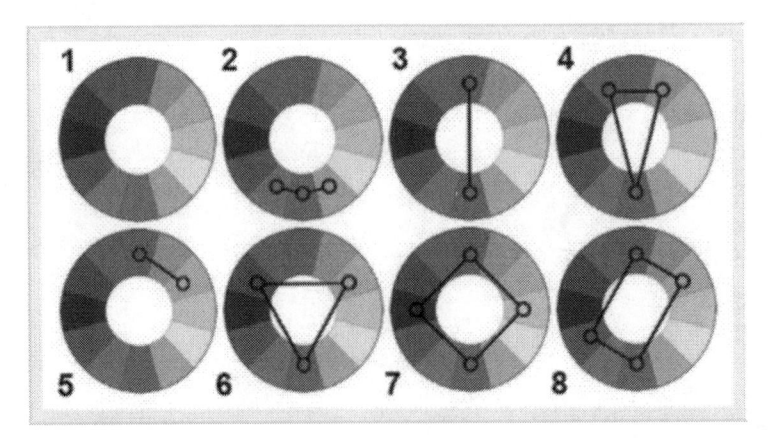

If you don't have an Itten circle, make use of different apps and websites for selecting ready-made color solutions.

Examples of assistant sites:

1. https://colorscheme.ru/ (online color wheel).

With the help of the online circle, we select harmonious color combinations.

Select a color on the color wheel. The program automatically selects all the shades you can use with the selected color on the right. On the top left, you see all the schemes of color harmonies with the color you are interested in.

2. color.romanuke.com (ready-made palettes with pictures). Colors harmonize with each other in the form of a picture and a palette.

Also, we can always observe nature, and it will not deceive us. All the colors found in nature are 100% in harmony. Nature's palette has no mistakes. You can also see the color palette on Pinterest.

Before starting, it's important to think about the theme and color scheme. Imagine at once what final result needs to be achieved. The painter puts his emotions into his paintings, and the stronger the emotion, the more it is transmitted to those around him.

❖ *Johannes Itten's book "The Art of Color" - more color information.*

Color affects people physiologically. Some colors can be calming, and others can activate or make us feel comfortable. Pale, unsaturated hues and the predominance of cool hues make us feel broody. Warm, saturated tones create a more upbeat, cheerful mood.

When choosing a color scheme for your work, don't forget to take into account:

-peculiarities of the room (small or large space) where the picture will be located;

-peculiarities of personal perception of color;

-the meaning and properties of each color.

Below, we use the brief **meaning and properties of colors** as a little hint.

Red is the color of fire and passion. It is a bold, energetic, and lively color that symbolizes confidence, strength, and power. Bright accents of red, for example, in the bedroom are recommended by sexologists, but they should not be intrusive; tiny dots of red will do perfectly.

Orange is the color of freshness, creativity, youth, and energy. This color is ideal for small rooms where there is little natural light. Since it is an appetite-exciting color, it is suitable for dining rooms and kitchens.

Yellow is the color of smiles, positivity, joy, and light. Paintings with yellow color will visually add volume to small rooms. Use this color for children's rooms as well.

Blue means coolness, freshness, openness, and freedom. We use this color in offices. Blue means reliability, sociability, and openness. This color has a calming effect on a person. It helps one to fall asleep quickly, but it suppresses passion. Blue is preferred in relaxation and meditation rooms. The deeper the blue color, the stronger it awakens the desire for purity in a person.

For an English-speaking audience, blue can mean depression, as there is an English expression "to be blue," which means "to be upset, to be sad," but this is not always the case.

Green is the color of nature, the color of life, ecology, wealth, and prestige. Paintings in a dark green palette represent prestige, wealth, and abundance (malachite).

Purple is spirituality, mystery, and extravagance. It is the color of art, the color of women. Purple will look good in living rooms, but place it with special care in bedrooms and dining rooms as it can curb appetite and desire.

Turquoise is an extravagant color, the color of life. However, this incredibly saturated shade can be psychologically crushing if it is in excess, so it is recommended to dilute this color.

Pink (purple) - inner freedom, security, innocence, sentimentality, and romance. This color is a symbol of youth and creativity.

Brown is a simple, calm color that evokes a sense of material security and self-confidence. It is the color of sanity, business, and stability. Earth tones can be used in any room.

Gray is a neutral color. It is believed that this color can help relieve stress by being practical and calm.

Black is the color of luxury, sophistication, and grief. Black combines well with gold and white flowers.

White - symbolizes purity, innocence, goodness, life, and minimalism. Using it with the visual expansion of the room makes the room light. The transparency and perfection of this color always look winning. A painting with more white will emphasize brevity, minimalism, simplicity, and luxury. Works made on dark surfaces with white ink will look very contrasting.

Gold is not only a symbol of luxury - it is considered the color of health, optimism, and vitality.

Silver is soothing, sensual, and mysterious. It is the embodiment of politeness, wealth, and restraint.

Bronze - a touch of luxury. Flawless in ethnic style, ultra-modern soft, eclectic, modern, and minimalist.

Every year, PANTONE colors are defined. With such a good hint, you can consider fashion trends in art and design and apply them to your work https://www.pantone.com/eu/en/.

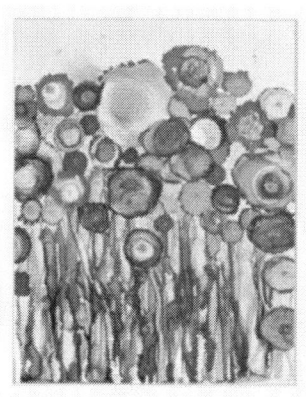

12. CREATING SKETCHES

A sketch is a quick drawing with a storyboard in color, shape, and dynamics to create harmonious pictures. This approximate form of presentation of the future work will be very convenient for the customer and you. The sketch shows us about 70% of the future work.

Such sketches go along with several techniques, where the ink is subjected to some control, such as deducing the loop of ink and drawing subject works (nature, animals, etc.). It is impossible to do such a sketch with a filler because the ink moves uncontrollably.

The sketch is made on a separate sheet of paper using pencils, pens, or alcohol markers.

Applying the rules and laws of composition (see chapter 10), we divide the sketch into 9 equal squares (rule of thirds). Arrange the drawing on the sketch so that it is balanced relative to the center.

The sketch shows us the future picture's dynamics, shape, and colors. We line up the shape in the drawing. It helps us prepare for the final work by giving us an understanding of where we are starting from, what colors we will use, etc.

Avoid symmetry in the paintings. For example, we start the painting on the right, and the touchpoint will be either slightly above or slightly below the painting. This dynamic will give the painting a distinctive look.

You can also draw intuitively, without a sketch.

13. COLORING BOOK. SKETCHBOOK

A coloring books. What's it for?

A sketchbook is an art journal with your ideas, drawings, and guide.

There is an extensive color palette of alcohol ink. When creating a new painting, we choose colors in advance. As a rule, the color is not the same on the cap or label of the ink. So you have to test the ink every time and see if a given color is right or wrong. Alcohol ink from different manufacturers differs when it dries.

Such sketchbooks are handy for artists. They are made for quick selection of the palette of the future painting and for revealing the chosen color on the surface.

You can also see how the ink will interact with each other.

As I do. Example:

I drop ink and alcohol on small pieces of synthetic paper, then blow it out with a hairdryer, and dry this drop. This is how I make the ink drop. When you mix the ink and alcohol, you can see how the color unfolds.

To create a sketchbook, **you need:**

1. Purchase any sketchbook with black (white) pages of rectangular (square) size on a spring. This way, your sketchbooks

will look more effective.

2. Cut small shapes (squares, rectangles, or circles) from synthetic paper for coloring. Cut as many cards as you have ink colors.

3. We make the ink on the cut pieces of synthetic paper.

4. Sign the name, number, and brand of the ink beautifully on the ink.

5. We glue in the coloring, leaving room for a signature if necessary.

6. Make mini paintings using two or three colors of ink. Write down the colors used. Such paintings allow you to display the interaction of ink with each other.

When using the coloring cards, you will immediately see what can be combined with what, focusing on the Itten circle.

Don't forget to keep the proportions of color (60-30-10). With the help of coloring cards, you will see which color will be the dominant and which color will be the accent.

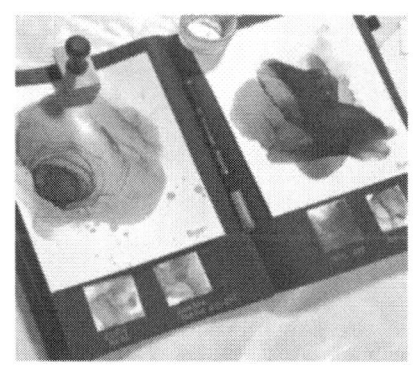

I have coloring books that are not pasted into a sketchbook. Such coloring cards are also handy for simplifying communication with clients. They are also handy for quickly finding a color scheme for a future painting.

14. PROTECTION OF PAINTINGS. VARNISHES

Upon completion, all work with alcoholic inks must be coated with a protective layer, namely a varnish. I have written before that lightfastness is an essential characteristic of alcohol ink.

Alcohol-based inks are translucent, so you shouldn't leave your work unprotected from direct sunlight. Over time, the paintings will lose their durability, and some may disappear altogether. Also, the ink can blur, change color, or become faded when filled with epoxy. Therefore, protect such paintings so they won't burn out.

One method of protecting a painting with alcohol ink is to coat it with water-based acrylic varnish for artwork.

There are glossy, matte, satin, and semi-matt acrylic varnishes on the market. How to apply an aerosol varnish correctly:

- Dry the work thoroughly. Leave the work for a couple of hours, and dry the wet areas with a hairdryer.
- Spray the first layer of protective varnish on the picture while standing 30-40 cm from the picture. Allow the painting to dry for one hour.
- Repeat the procedure one or two more times.
- Cover your work with protective film so that dust particles do not remain on it.
- Spray UV spray varnish on your artwork in 2 to 3 coats while drying between coats.

The wrong spray varnish can blur your ink, completely change the opposite color, or the color of the ink on the work will become faded.

The most suitable water-based aerosol varnishes for spirit ink work are:

1. **Pebeo Vernis a Tableau Mat acrylic spray varnish** (orange label). Available in gloss, matte, and satin.

Creates the perfect finish for your works. The lacquer does not have a strong odor compared to other varnishes. The lacquer has good hiding power, and the ink does not change color; it is not washed out when coated.

The disadvantage is the absence of UV protection. If necessary, you must take an additional UV varnish.

2.**Krylon's Kamar® Varnish. UV Protectant (Krylon® UV-Resistant Clear Coating**, Golden® Archival Varnish with UVLS or other). It is a UV-free and UV-protective finish varnish. This means that it will not be damaged by UV light.

3. **Cons:** It has a strong odor. Consumption of Krylon varnish is higher than that of other varnishes. It is not recommended to work with such aerosol varnish without a mask, goggles, and a very ventilated room.

❖ *You can't apply UV lacquer immediately because the lacquer interacts with the ink.*

4. **Acrylic spray varnish Montana Gold.**
There are glossy and matte lacquers.
They create a perfect coating for your works, have good hiding power, and the ink does not change color and does not blur when coating.
Pros: UV protection. The lacquer contains UV filters that protect your painting from fading. Excellent hiding power, colors are retained, do not change, and do not fade when adequately applied! When you apply a matte Montana varnish, you can't see the dust that might settle on your painting after drying.
Cons: It has a strong odor. There is a reaction with some inks - the colors fade and change their shade. Working with such aerosol varnish is not recommended without a mask, goggles, and a ventilated room. It is better to work with such a varnish on the street.

5. Golden acrylic spray varnish.

There are matte, satin, and gloss lacquers from this company.

Coating with a glossy acrylic varnish will make the color of the ink appear brighter. A matte acrylic varnish will give a velvety feel. Nude ink colors are also better covered with a matte acrylic varnish.

❖ *A large amount of acrylic varnish on the ink can cause the ink to move, as the UV varnish contains alcohol. Therefore, spray the varnish gradually and at 30-40 cm from the picture. Spray the aerosol varnish from edge to edge to fill the picture area.*

The second method of protecting paintings is framing the painting under glass. Glass also protects the ink from fading. However, before framing your painting under glass, protect it with UV varnish.

The third method of protecting paintings is to coat them with transparent epoxy resin. Before pouring the epoxy resin, protect the paintings in the ink technique with UV varnish according to the abovementioned rules. If the painting is not covered with a protective UV varnish, the ink may blur a little, and the precise edges will turn into a blurred composition.

❖ *Some inks change color under the epoxy, so be sure to cover with several layers of protective varnish and dry the picture.*

You can learn more about epoxy resin from my book "A Step-by-Step Guide to Resin" (see Ch. 9 for a link to the book).

The fourth method of protecting paintings is copies of your art, prints, giclee prints, and laser printing. The shelf life of such works will be more than 100 years. Printed copies can be made on canvas, glossy paper, ceramics, silk, fabric, and metal. There can be different sizes.

We scan and print in professional workshops where the quality will be high. Quality printing of your work can be confused with the original.

How to take care of alcohol ink paintings.

1. Do not hang alcohol ink paintings in direct sunlight or under any heating device. If you do, over time, your ink will simply fade.

2. If the painting has no glass, dust such paintings with a dry cloth or dust broom.

❖ *In natural conditions - proper humidity, air temperature, and no direct sunlight, your paintings will remain in their original form for a long time.*

❖ *The thickness of the paper helps to slow down the fading of the design because the paper itself holds more ink.*

15. CONDENSAT

Condensation appears in works when the alcohol loses its physical and chemical properties or when there is high humidity outside. The ink begins to peel and leaves a greasy, oily track or torn, ribbed edges on the work. Another way to put it is that the alcohol gives a dirty edge. Water gets into the alcohol, and it is challenging to dry such paths afterward.

With quality alcohol, the ink with the alcohol will be unified, without delamination, and the edges will be smooth and beautiful.

Condensation can also be turned into a beautiful effect.

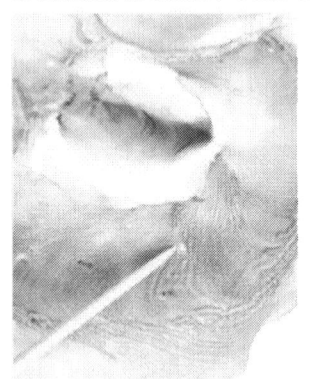

Alcohol Recommendations:
- Avoid extreme temperatures with alcohol. Don't draw with alcohol ink in the heat! There will be many defects due to rapid evaporation and condensation.
- All alcohols are sensitive to temperature changes. The temperature in the room with the alcohol is about 20 degrees.
- Do not keep alcohol open. Close the alcohol bottle tightly at all times (even when working).
- Avoid direct sunlight when working with alcohol.

16. WORK PROCESS. HAND POSITIONING

Working with alcohol ink will almost always be the same irrespective of the technique. Remember, a hairdryer is an essential tool in working with alcohol ink. The hairdryer has a switch - air control. We almost always work on the first air control mode.

The principles of the ink and hairdryer are as follows:

We form a stain with ink, dry it, add another stain (even going over ready-made stains), dry it again gradually form a composition. We add second stain to the colored one, and so on until all the elements of the painting are in harmony.

As I do. Example:

I put on gloves and a mask. I prepare the workplace by covering it with tape. I tape the synthetic paper to the surface.

1. I wipe the sheet of paper with alcohol on which I'm going to draw. If the paper's surface is clean, the ink will be even, and there will be no streaks. I wipe with a napkin soaked in alcohol (this is how

you remove invisible dust that settles in the process from the sheet of paper).

2. Adding color (alcohol ink). I take the Copic "Cardinal" ink R59 (3 drops) and drip it on the diagonal. Then I add a little Ranger "Stream" ink.

The amount of ink depends on the idea of the drawing and the chosen color.

❖ *If your idea is to fill the entire surface, you will need to drop more ink.*
❖ *If you want to see more air (white space in the picture), you'll need less ink accordingly.*

❖ In the lessons below, I describe the amount of alcohol and the color of the ink. As you create your paintings, you will intuitively understand the amount of alcohol and ink needed.

❖ *Lighter shades of ink usually have higher consumption rates than darker shades. Darker colors can be diluted with alcohol to produce more shades.*

❖ *If you apply light ink with alcohol at the beginning, the color of the ink will not show well on the surface, but as the ink dries, you will be able to see the color unfold.*

3. Next, I add isopropanol around one side of the ink and the other. The amount of alcohol depends on the idea and the size of the surface.

4. Blow on the ink to combine with the alcohol and unfolds.

Add metallics if desired. Since metallics are heavier than alcohol ink, they will settle on the surface. Spread the metallics over the surface with your finger, mixing a little with the ink.

The metallics will remain a solid metallic smudge when dry if you don't.

5. I spread the ink spot with a stream of air (the hairdryer is on the first speed) over the entire area, creating a shape.

I dry slowly and hold the hairdryer perpendicular to the sheet (right angle) at 30-40 cm from the drawing without tilting it.

❖ *At the beginning of the work, we see a solid spot of ink, but if you're patient, you'll see a pattern form.*

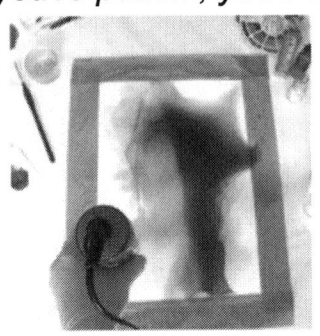

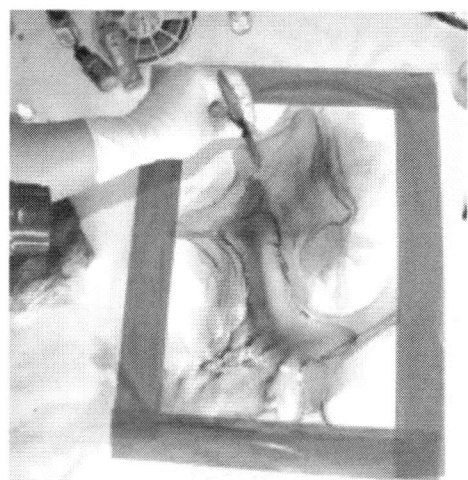

6. I move the hairdryer around the surface circularly away from the picture. I blow on the ink spot from all sides, directing the air currents only along the edges, avoiding the center. I change the position of the hairdryer and control the spot, moving it intuitively.

7. I run a hairdryer over the entire surface (the perimeter of all sides) so that no drops form. Using the airflow and its direction, I form a lovely spot.

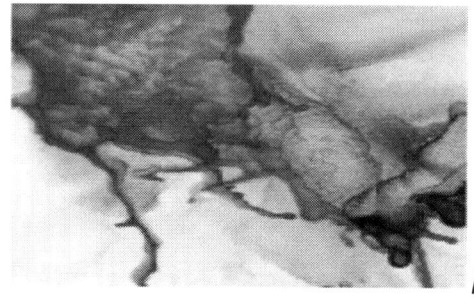

❖ *Pointing the hairdryer into the center of the picture will cause all the ink to mix and splatter in different directions.*

❖ *The sharper the angle of the hairdryer, the faster the ink runs off, forming runs or so-called worms.*

7. Next, I add color, Ranger "Stream," and *blow the color spot (ink) around the perimeter on all sides.*

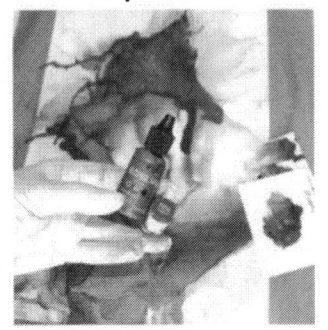

❖ When you mix inks, they give a different shade. When I combined my shades, I got a cool purple.
❖ Before working, test the interaction of the ink with each other on a separate sheet of synthetic paper.

9. I don't stop working - I don't turn off the hairdryer in the middle of an un-dried element. I use a hairdryer to the end of each element in work; otherwise, there will be oily, torn edges.

❖ The picture can be rasterized. Turn the picture to the right, to the left, turn it upside down and see which *version you like best. According to the composition, cut off unnecessary parts.*

10. I fix the picture with a protective varnish. I let the picture dry for 24 hours.

11. I am framing the picture.

- ❖ *Remember that the color spot takes longer to dry than warm (hot) airflow with cold airflow.*
- ❖ *Remember about human visual perception of color spots in the picture - darker shades in the center and lighter shades - on the edges.*
- ❖ *The color spot on the right has more weight than the spot on the left.*

17. TECHNIQUES FOR WORKING WITH ALCOHOL INK

Lesson 1: Practical part. Getting to know the technique of drawing with alcohol ink

Alcohol ink is a unique material with which you can create and decorate many exciting things.

Working with alcohol ink seems simple, but it requires a lot of practice and skill. Don't be afraid of disappointments; try to experiment, find something new for yourself and enjoy your actions because ink knows how to surprise you!

Before you work, make sure the table you draw is level; otherwise, all the ink will roll to one side.

In the beginning, play a little with the ink, see how it opens up to you and what it can do when it interacts with alcohol.

You can draw with ink either "wet" or "dry. This means you apply a layer of alcohol to a clean sheet of synthetic paper with a container before you work, then draw on that base.

The "wet-on-wet" technique means you don't wait for the alcohol to dry but draw immediately with a brush and ink without a hairdryer.

The basic rules of such an admission:

Fill the entire surface of the sheet with alcohol and apply different colors of alcohol ink in a chaotic pattern closer to the center. You can apply the ink in stripes, dots, strokes, wavy lines, etc.

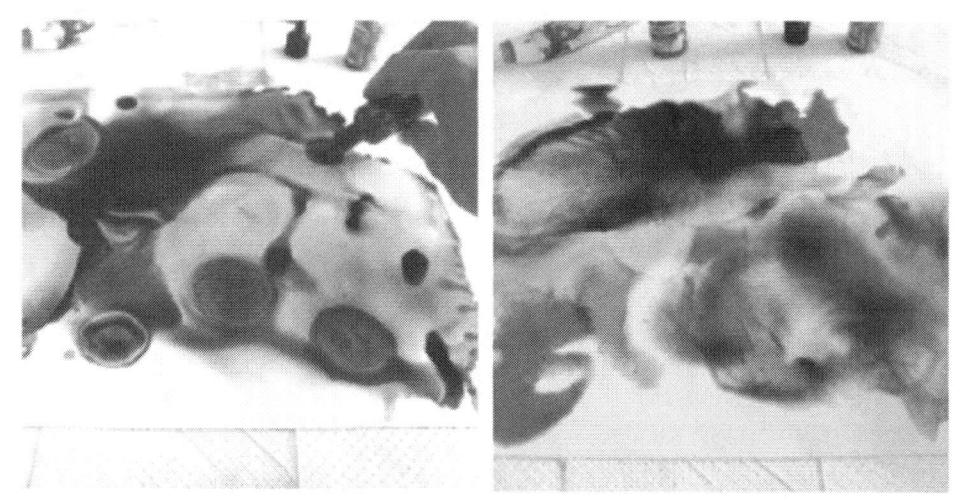

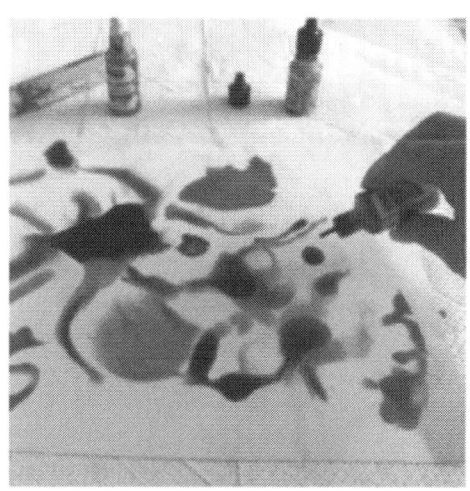

Blow them out, and let the ink of different colors join together by tilting the surface in different directions.

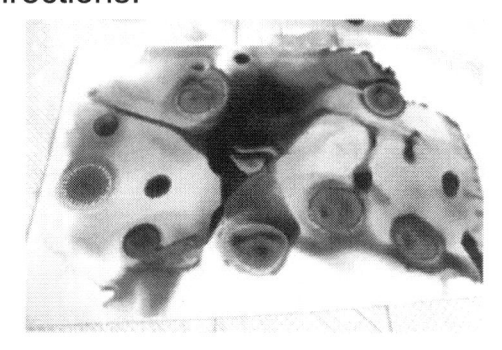

Then take a darker ink than the previous one and drip randomly on the same surface until the alcohol is dehydrated. On a wet surface, the dark drops of ink will disperse.

As I do. Example:

1. I prepare my workplace (oilcloth, alcohol, ink, a brush, a rubber tip, a hairdryer, a bottle with a sharp end, a roll of tissues, and synthetic paper).
2. Sometimes, I attach the synthetic paper to the table's surface with scotch tape on all sides.
3. I think through the idea of my drawing. You can draw a sketch, determine the approximate direction of the ink, or do it intuitively.
4. I choose colors for the work to be done and look at the interaction of colors on paper with alcohol and when mixing. My colors are selected. I use Itten's circle as an assistant.
5. I wipe the surface of the paper with alcohol from dust.
6. Then, I fill the surface with alcohol so that the alcohol does not have time to dry.
7. I immediately apply any ink to the surface in stripes and dots, alternating them.
8. I inflate the ink so that they all connect, tilting the surface in different directions.
9. I wait about 5 seconds for the ink to open completely. The alcohol evaporates slightly from the surface (remember, the alcohol must not dry out completely!).
10. Then, I take the accent color of the ink and randomly apply drops to the surface.
11. On a wet surface, the dark drops of ink will diverge in exciting ways, creating an image that looks like space or the bottom of the ocean.
12. I use a "fan" brush to connect the dark ink in some places.
13. Here we have such an attractive surface, which can be used for collage, paintings, or to make a painting on a wooden base with

decorative paste and epoxy. More about that will come in other lessons below.

The "dry technique" means you paint with a hairdryer or other aids (compressor, pear, tube, etc.).

The basic rules of this technique:

Apply the ink to the surface in stripes, dots, strokes, wavy lines - whatever you like.

Take a bottle of alcohol and blur the ink in different directions; let it flow and mix.

Add metallics (gold, silver) if desired. Spread the metallic over the surface with your finger, mixing a little of it with the ink. Since metallics are heavier than alcohol ink, they will settle on the surface.

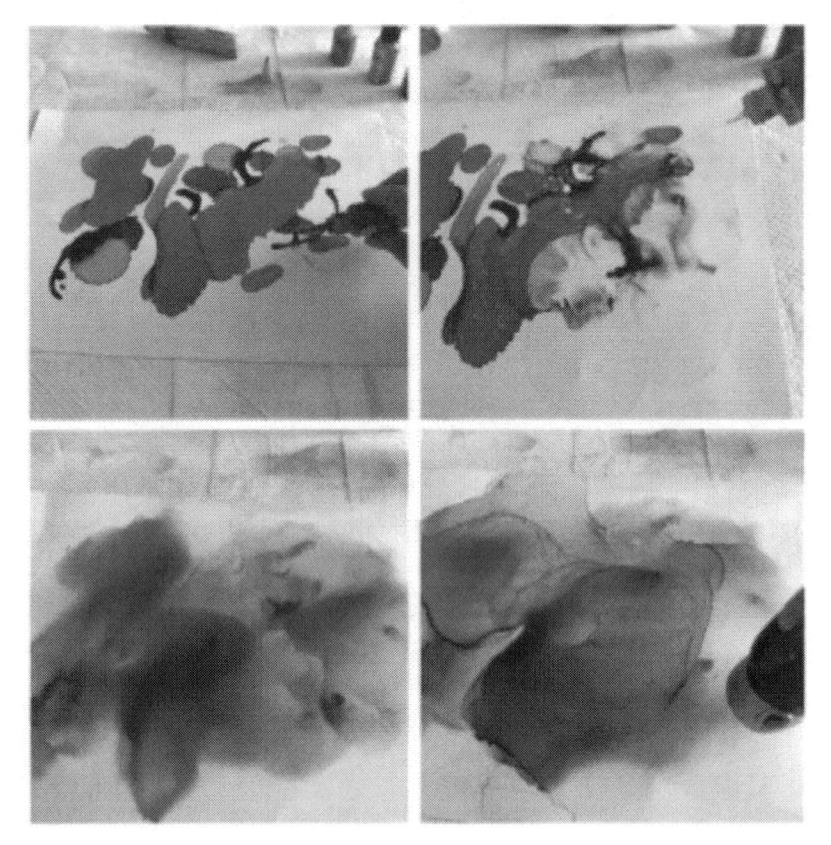

Turn on the hairdryer to medium power, holding it perpendicular to the paper. Blow the color spot (ink) around the perimeter on all sides. The hairdryer is your brush. Draw with a stream of air, smoothly and gently, moving from the edges to the center. Don't stay in one place for too long; otherwise, the drawing won't be exciting, and the paper may deform slightly from the warm air.

By adding more alcohol, you can stretch the color and finish the edge gently. Or, conversely, add more ink, depending on whether you want to make the spot darker or lighter.

Make "worms" blotches by blowing a hairdryer into the center of the spot; see if you like that effect. Or, on the contrary, add more alcohol and use the airflow and its direction to form an excellent stain.

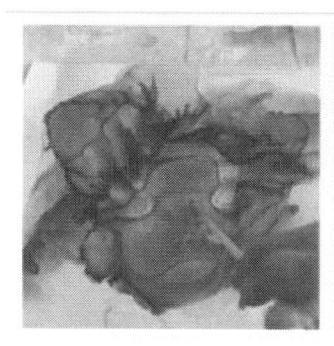

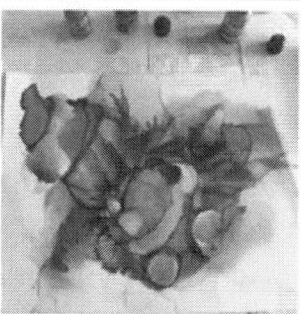

As I do. Example:

1. I prepare my workplace (oilcloth, alcohol, ink, a brush, a rubber tip, a hairdryer, a bottle with a sharp end, a roll of tissues, and synthetic paper).
2. I glue the synthetic paper to the surface with scotch tape on all sides.
3. I think through the approximate direction of the ink.
4. I choose colors for future work and look at the interaction of colors on paper with alcohol and mixing.
5. I wipe the surface of the paper with alcohol from dust.
6. I immediately apply ink and some alcohol to the surface in stripes and dots, alternating them.
8. I fan the ink to join together, tilting the surface in different directions with a hairdryer.

Don't be afraid to mess up a blank sheet of paper. You can permanently remove the extra element or wipe off the entire drawing with a napkin if something goes wrong.

❖ *You can improve your drawing skills with alcohol ink by practicing daily, by "cupping" your hand.*

Lesson 2: Monochrome Technique

Monochromatic harmony (monochrome) always looks advantageous.

It is a combination of the same color in different degrees of saturation. Remember that each color is used in a different degree of saturation on the Itten color wheel, from dark to light.

As I do. Example:

I pour plenty of alcohol (iso) on synthetic paper and apply undiluted ink of one color to the undried surface. I apply the ink in a snaking pattern. I use Copic "Toner Gray" T10 ink.

I spread the ink spot with a stream of air (hair dryer on speed one) over the entire area, creating a beautiful shape. I dry slowly, gently, giving direction to the pattern.

Your task is to create a beautifully shaped drawing while making it dynamic.

When you blow out a color (ink) stain, it is essential to watch the direction of the stain. To keep your composition intact, adjust the direction of the air (tilt of the blow dryer) where your stain will flow.

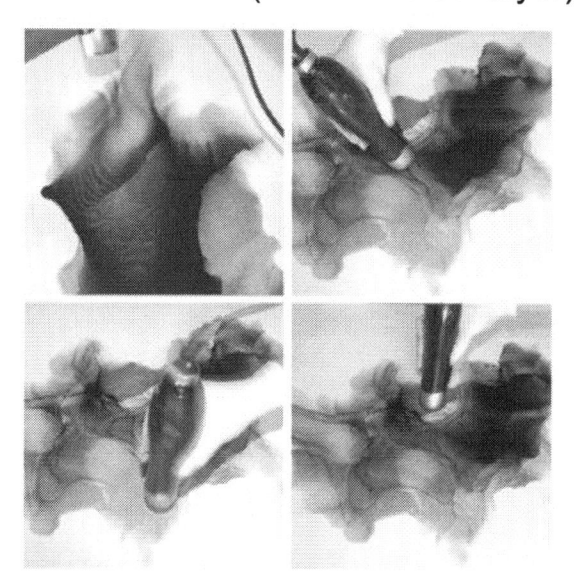

When we work from edge to edge, the peculiarity is that ink accumulates at the edge, and should be removed. This can be done by directing the airflow from the hairdryer, driving the ink down a bit (toward the center of the painting), or using paper to collect the excess ink.

At the end of the job, when there is a spot of color left over, use the hairdryer in a circular motion. This way, you finish the work and get beautiful edges.

At the end of the painting, fix it with a matte varnish. Allow the work to dry (see chapter 14 for details). Frame the work.

COPIC ·TONER GRAY· T10

Lesson 3: Drawing on Canvas

There is a big difference between drawing with ink on synthetic paper and drawing on canvas. In the latter case, you will need to prepare a primed canvas. The primer is needed to prevent ink from penetrating the canvas, close the material's pores, and give a uniform density and absorbency to the entire surface.

If the canvas is not primed, it is necessary to prime it in 2 to 3 layers and let it dry completely (one day) before starting the work.

Choose a fine-grained, primed canvas. There are wedges on the back of the canvas that you can use to tap and stretch the canvas to the desired tension.

There are several options for applying ink to canvas:
- spread the ink with a brush across the canvas, color by color;
- pour diluted alcohol ink on the canvas, color by color;
- apply undiluted ink to the canvas, add alcohol, and blow it out with a hairdryer.

As I do. Example:

I apply Ranger "Stonewashed" ink and Copic "Flash Pink" E95 ink on the primed cotton canvas.

I add a diagonal gold metallic. This will give the picture a beautiful shimmer (before spreading the metallic on the canvas, you need to shake the cup because metallics settle as they are heavier than conventional inks).

I mix a little ink with a hairdryer on the first speed so there are no clear transitions between the colors. Then I repeat the process, immediately blowing out the next color of ink. Eventually, the entire space should be filled with ink.

Observe how beautifully the ink interacts with the metallics. You can leave the work to dry on its own or dry the ink with a hair dryer.

The choice is yours.

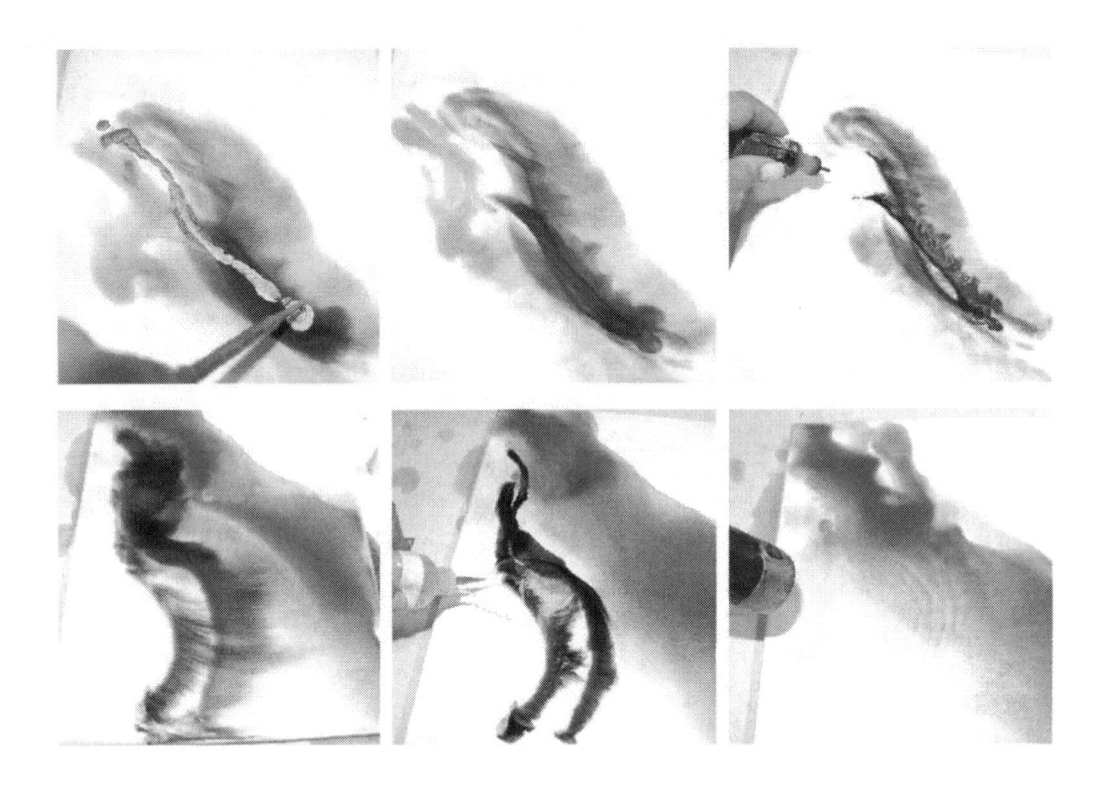

Next, I apply Copic "Night Blue" B97 ink, giving a diagonal composition. I add alcohol all over the strip and spread the ink with an air stream. I add more alcohol and dry the work slowly to create beautiful soft gradients.

I apply white pigment in some places. It is desirable to apply it on a wet surface so it is not quickly absorbed into the surface of the canvas.

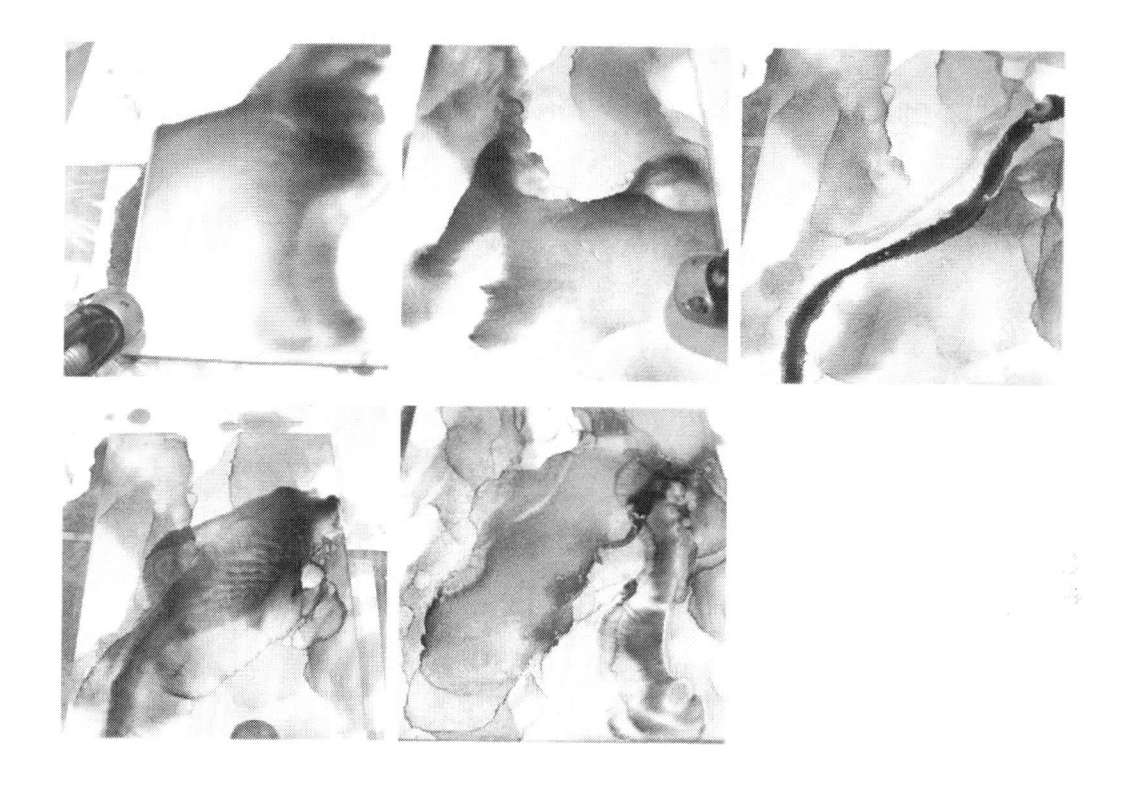

After the painting dries, I cover the surface with UV varnish.

The last step is framing the painting. An adequately chosen baguette transforms the picture. The colors look brighter, and the picture itself looks more solid.

❖ On dark surfaces, add white or pearlescent pigments to the regular ink; otherwise, the ink will not be visible against the dark background.

A few recommendations for choosing a baguette:

1. The baguette should match the picture in color, taking the cold and warm shades into account.
2. The colors of the baguette should be half a tone darker or lighter than the primary color in the picture.
3. Paintings made with alcoholic ink are more suitable for modern frames.
4. Small paintings look more effective in wide baguettes. That way, you focus the viewer's eye on the painting itself.

Take into account the style of the painting. A modern painting in a classic molding with stucco would be out of place. Simple, laconic, glossy baguettes are suitable for modern paintings.

Lesson 4: The technique of drawing "on the plum. Fleur."

Fleur is a thin silk fabric. Fleur paintings are similar to silk; they are just as weightless and transparent but can also be lush and bright. More, "fleur" translated to English means a flower. These are the petals we will draw with alcohol ink.

Prepare synthetic paper, alcohol ink (4 colors), disposable medical diapers, and alcohol. You can use 96.6% ethanol in this technique.Determine the composition and color scheme of the painting. Make a sketch beforehand, determining the direction of your petals. Practice on a small section of the draft, and sharpen your movements.

Take a piece of synthetic paper and place it tilted over a table covered with medical diapers. Pour ink (3-4 colors) over the middle of the edge of the paper and pour alcohol from the beginning of the petal. Tilt the sheet of paper, so the excess ink drains onto the medical diaper.

When you tilt a sheet of paper in different directions, the ink and the alcohol will flow (drain) down. That's why working with this technique is called "pouring." To keep the edges of the petal closer to the end of the work from tearing and forming dark borders, add more alcohol from the beginning of the work.

Add some ink (3–4 colors) and pour the alcohol back onto the sheet. Alcohol going into the already formed pattern blurs it so that the petals become like silk. Beautiful borders between petals and interesting color transitions appear. If you want a pronounced petal shade, add more ink in the color you want.

Distribute the petals over the entire surface of the sheet of paper. You can change the direction of the petals slightly - this will add expressiveness to the picture.

You can direct a spot of color and give direction to the plum by tilting and bending the paper. The petals are not straight, which gives the picture dynamics.

Petals can also be dried with a hairdryer when the ink has spread over the surface and flowed down. It is possible to work on a drain without simply a hair dryer. Dry the spots by directing the airflow tangentially, tilting the paper in the right direction, and forming a silky texture.

Don't be afraid to do layering on silky petals. If you don't like any element, put two drops of ink in two colors and add alcohol again to refresh that spot.

Since my painting turned out bright, I lightened it with alcohol spray. I poured alcohol into a sprayer and sprayed it on the work. A kind of holes was formed, which made the work as a whole lighter. After that, I used a brush to create droplets. I dipped the brush in alcohol and applied dots to the area I wanted.

❖ *Paintings in the "fleur-de-lis" technique on darker paper shades look very bright.*
❖ *When working on a dark surface, add white or pearlescent pigments.*
❖ *Works on large formats in the technique "on the drain" look more exciting and compelling.*

Lesson 5: Free Drying Techniques with a Hairdryer

1. Free drying WITHOUT hairdryer on synthetic paper.
Prepare the colors using alcohol ink. I have one color: Copic "Verdigris" G85. Randomly pour the alcohol and ink on the surface of the sheet of paper. Allow the ink to mix with the alcohol, fanning it out.

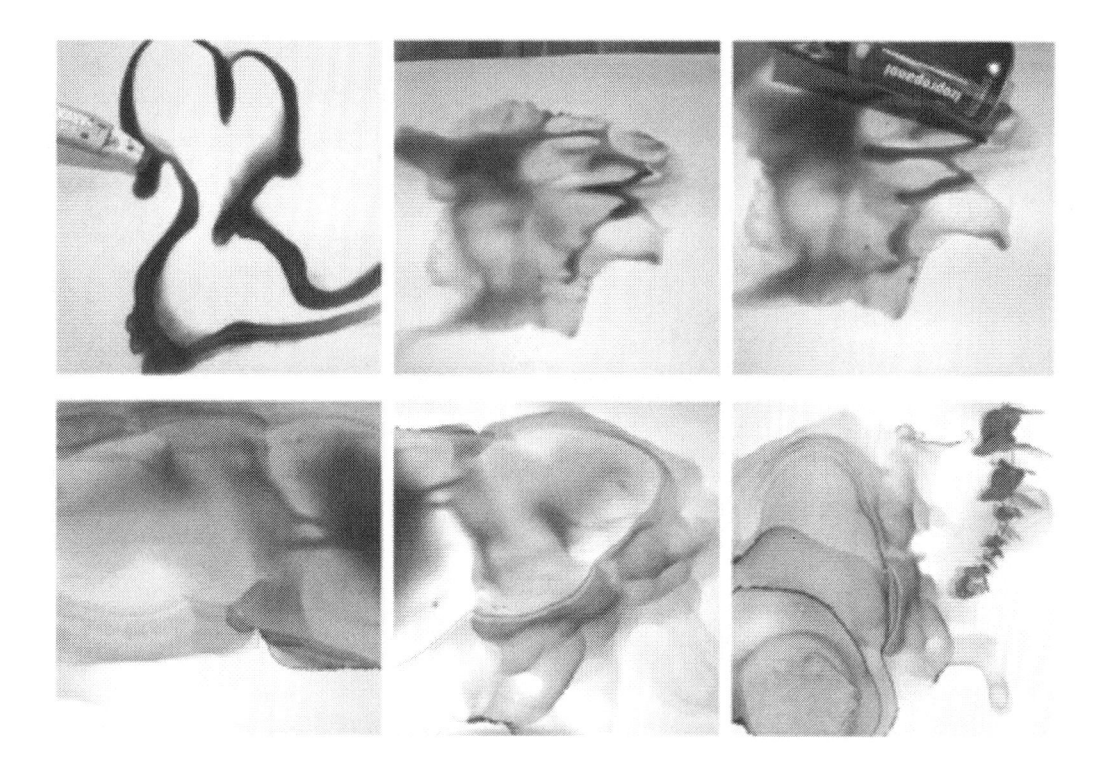

To keep the picture's edges from being stiff from the ink, pour in alcohol and blow again. Leave the surface to dry completely without your interference.

You will see how the ink dries on its own with absolutely no hairdryer, and beautiful fine edges appear on the paper's surface.

This picture dried in about 1 hour. The drying speed depends on the area to be poured.

❖ *Alcohol ink, when drying on its own, forms characteristic circles around areas of liquid accumulation, resembling indentations. The color spot dries faster where there is less ink but dries slower where there is a lot of ink, forming circles that resemble pits on paper.*

❖ *Distinct circles are characteristic of dye-based inks (marker refills); with pigmented inks, this effect is less pronounced or almost non-existent.*

To get a beautiful, precise edge in this technique, you should consider the following points:

- Use only clear ink.
- Do not add pearlescent pigments.
- Alcohol must be isopropyl alcohol. The higher the percentage of alcohol, the more obvious and even the edges will be.
- Work with the window ajar. This way, the airflow will help the alcohol to evaporate evenly. If there is no airflow in the room, the alcohol will evaporate evenly, and you will get a solid spot without edges.
- Room temperature operation is welcomed.
- The tablet must also be at room temperature.
- The ink should be free of sediment. The sediment prevents the appearance of facets. Exclude metallics and nacre. They are heavy and stain the surface.

Lesson 6: Marble backgrounds and stain effect. Splash effect

Marble Backgrounds.

Marble backgrounds can be the perfect wallpaper for your rooms, covers for diaries and notebooks, bookmarks, and cute cards for any holiday.

A dropper can help you with this technique. This is an alcohol bottle with a precise tip that helps you control where you pour the alcohol and how you move it. If you want to apply alcohol on a spot, this is very important.

As I do. Example:

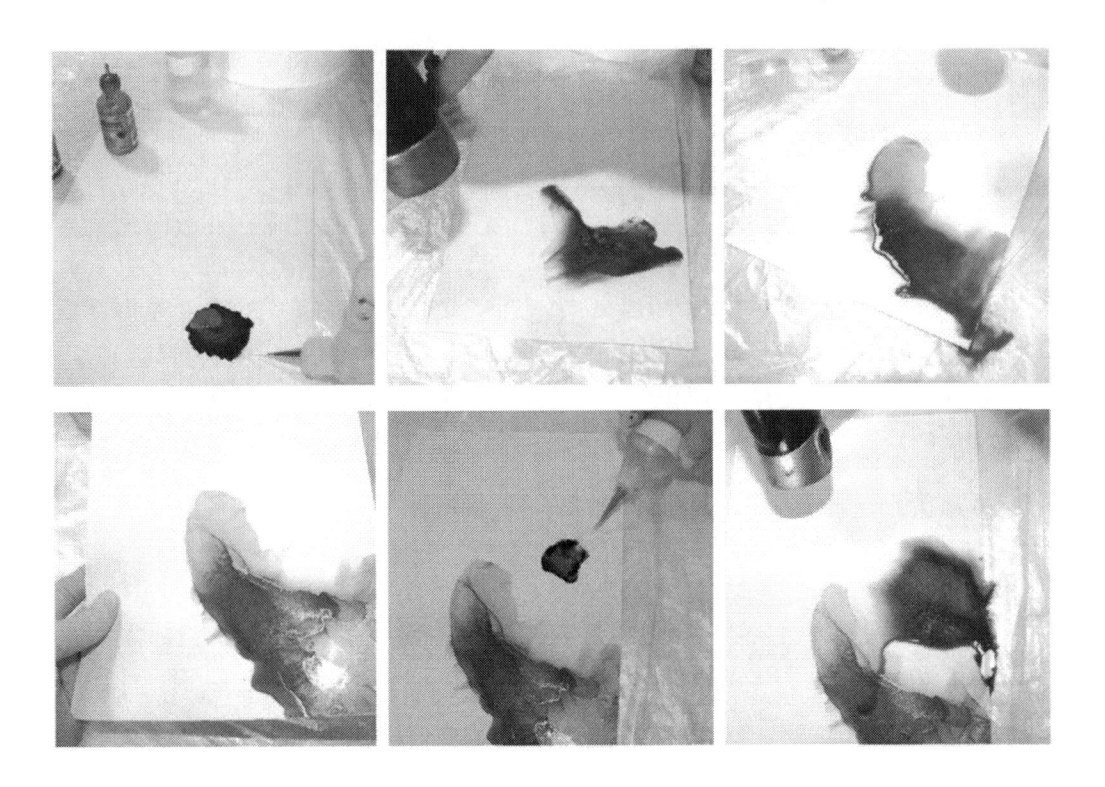

In this piece, I use Pinata Sangria and Pinata Gold alcohol ink. I put two drops of alcohol ink on the paper from the bottom right corner and one drop of metallic ink inside the color. On top of this significant drop, I pour alcohol with a dropper and start drying by blowing with a hairdryer at low speed.

The ink interacts with the metallics to create subtle veins of marble. Wherever you move the veins, do it so that they create an overall pattern.

After drying the pattern from one drop, make another drop and blow it over the surface in the same way with alcohol. Try to make the edge of the pattern light and the dark part closer to the center.

Adjust the width of the metal vein yourself. If you want to make even more pronounced veining, add more metallics.

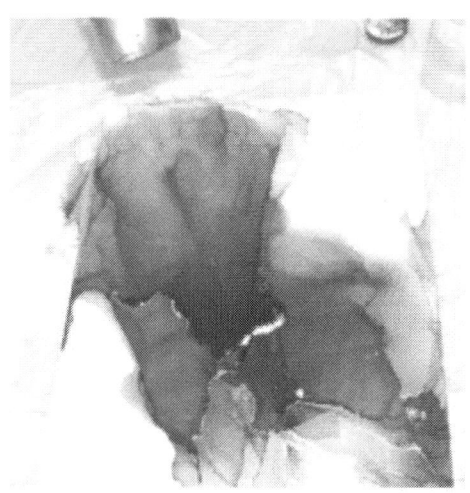

❖ *If you want to create a delicate marble with veining, you need to add two drops of alcohol ink in a glass with alcohol and pipette the color. Then apply it to the surface and blow it with a hairdryer with metallic ink.*

The secret to adding beautiful splashes

When working with alcohol ink, you can add different effects with splatters. Splatters, droplets, and holes (whichever you call them) come in different sizes. They are made with a sprayer with any alcohol (isopropanol, ethanol). They give airiness and lightness to work, and it is like a snow effect.

Position the spray at a distance of 25-30 cm from the surface of the drawing and make a few presses, then wait for a little. The drops do not appear immediately but after 2-3 seconds! Take your time to spray the same area several times. Spray from a distance; otherwise, your drops will be huge and may ruin your work.

You can also make splashes with a contrasting color. For example, bright pink ink splashes look bombastic on a blue background!

You don't have to make drops all over the work, and you can do it locally. For example, splashes are made in dark places to lighten the image.

How do you make splashes locally?

You cover the drawing area you would like to leave unchanged with paper.

Play around with different variations of color spots, and see how you can finish the work effectively where there is a lot of air.

Large droplets are easy to achieve with a regular brush dipped in alcohol. Shake off the alcohol a little and, tapping on your index finger with the brush, distribute the drops over the painting.

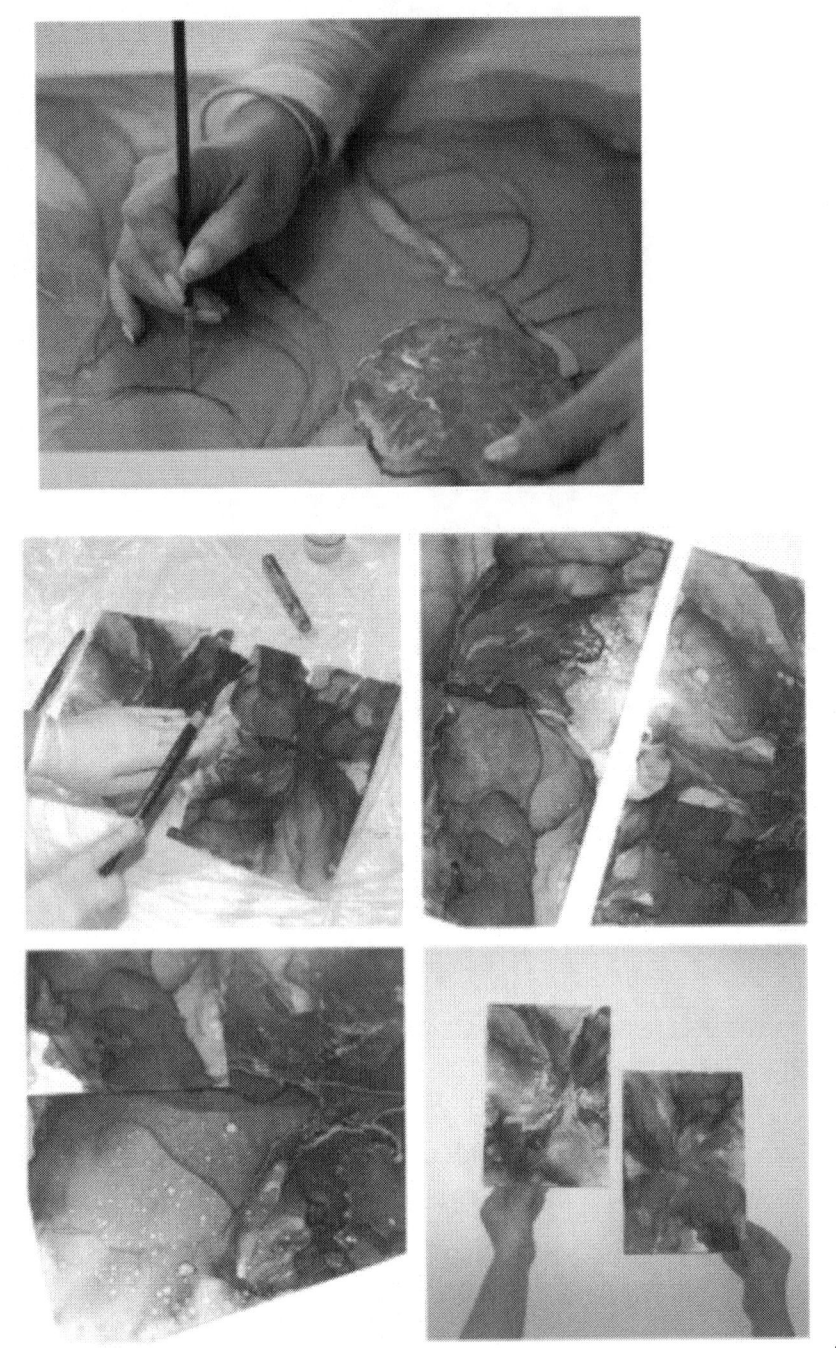

Tiny, beautiful droplets in scattering can be created with a brush - a fan, a regular brush. You can also make splashes with a contrasting color. This is the simple way to get an extra splatter effect.

❖ *To create the finished look of the design, apply the gold (silver) elements with a brush. You can always use a resin palette in the form of a cupholder to help—a convenient thing.*

Lesson 7. Gradients. Drawing in three or more colors

You must always be very careful when using three or more colors. The colors can blend so much that the picture becomes "dirty." That's why you should use a helper, the Itten circle.

In this lesson, I will show you how to work from a spot: to one spot, we join another, keeping the soft edges of the picture. My task is to use three colors to draw the shape of a circle in ink. It is better to prepare a large surface size. Build in the missing elements so that the picture looks balanced and coherent—finish drying before painting.

How I do it. Example:

I pour an alcohol puddle on the bottom right corner of a 50*70 cm synthetic paper and add the first ink (three drops). I add six to seven drops of alcohol. Make the entry soft, with no precise edges, and lead the color spot to the center with the hairdryer. The hairdryer is always on low speed.

When I have created part of the drawing, I add ink of a different color to the undried alcohol puddle. Don't create hard edges in the drawing. You can remove them with alcohol by blurring the edges and shaping the drawing with airflow.

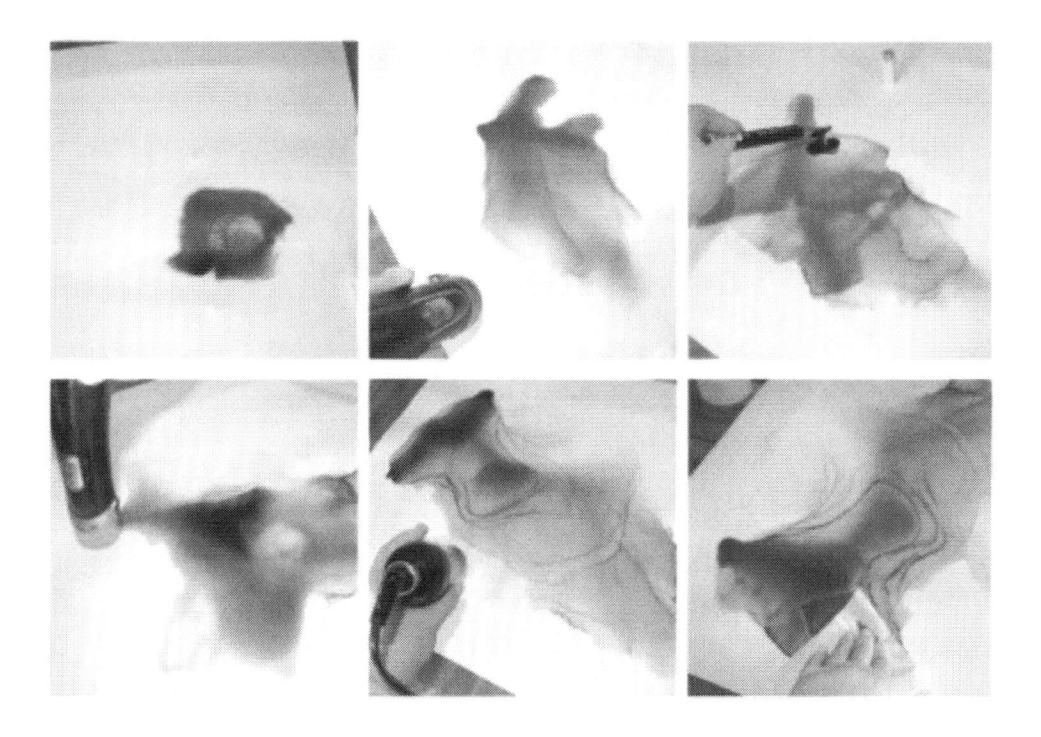

If you do not like something in the composition, remove the unnecessary elements with a napkin and alcohol and draw again. Then I blow the airflow of the color spot slightly toward the center in a circular motion in the form of a tunnel.

I make a soft entry into the drawing by adding alcohol and the third tone of ink to the undried puddle of color stain. I start blowing with a stream of air in a circular motion.

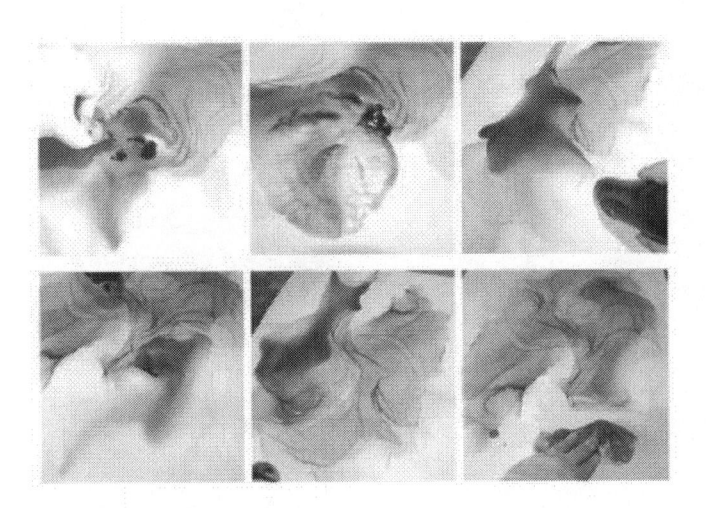

Some of the ink will blend toward the center, creating a fourth color that will look harmonious in combination with the others. Therefore, it is essential to choose the color scheme so that the picture will not be "dirty."

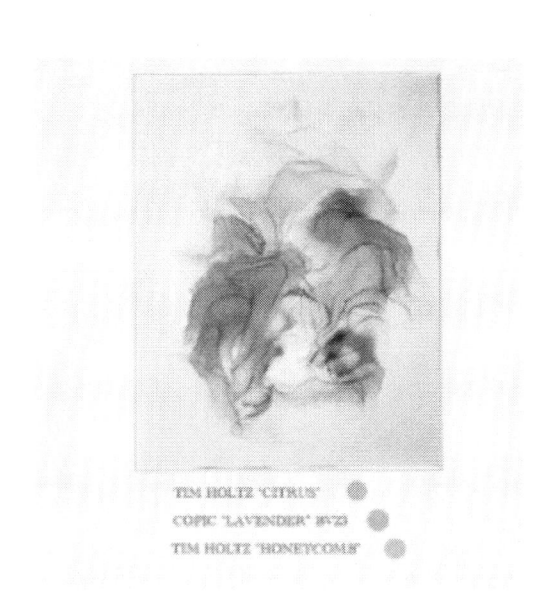

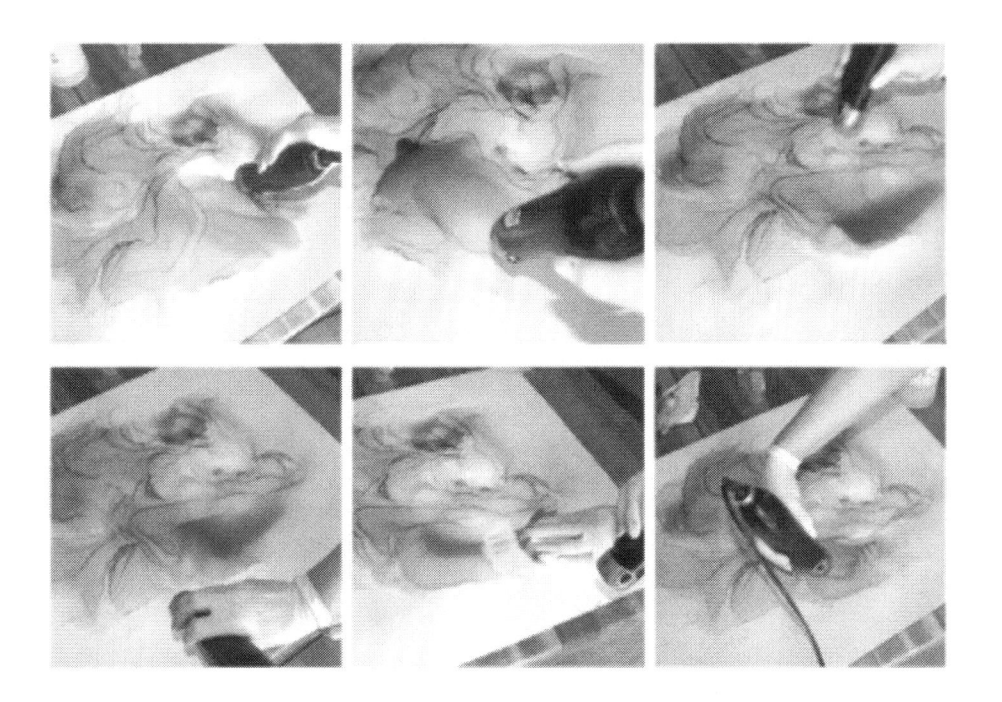

TIM HOLTZ 'CITRUS'
COPIC 'LAVENDER' #V23
TIM HOLTZ 'HONEYCOMB'

❖ *Alternate the ink, joining the finished stains, building into the overall pattern. Add alcohol to the edges where the edges are hard. Dry those edges tangentially with a hairdryer. By doing so, you will lighten the edges of the entry and achieve softness.*

Lesson 8: The "edge" or "plissé" technique

The principle of shaping elegant facets is simple. We apply ink in the form of a strip (Copic «Light Prawn» R22 and Copic «Process Blue» B05) to the surface, then pour alcohol on one side of the ink strip. Allow the ink to open and start blowing with a low-mode hairdryer.

It is essential to hold the hairdryer perpendicular to the surface: bring the hairdryer to the surface where the ink is and take it away; bring it in and take it away.

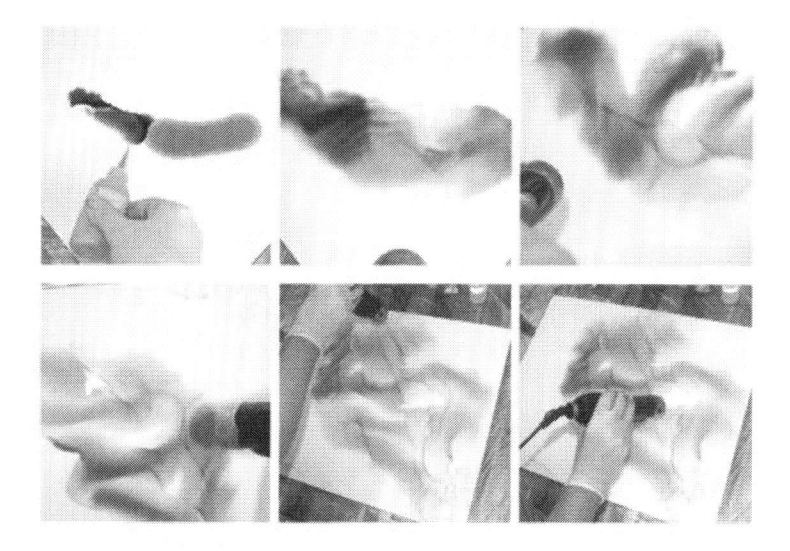

If you often move the hairdryer away from the ink spot, you get frequent, thin edges, or, in other words, a "plisse" effect, and on the contrary, if you hold the hairdryer long at the same distance from the ink spot, you get a wide edge.

If you take the hairdryer away for 2 seconds, uneven edges are formed. The longer the gap from the surface, the wider the edge will be. The more often you drive the hairdryer, the more often the edges (narrow edges) are formed.

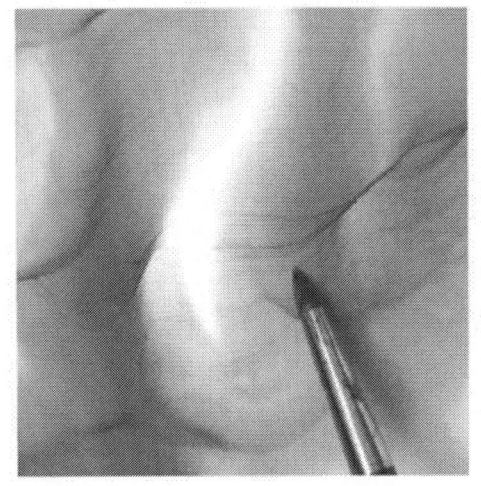

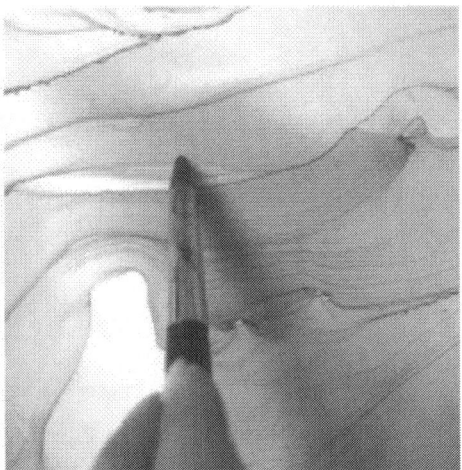

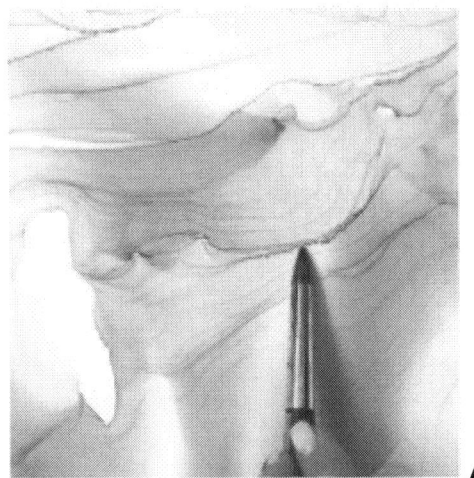

Again we bring the hairdryer to the surface, and the airflow will push the ink away, forming the edges. And so, bring the drawing to an end, adding ink and alcohol if necessary.

Using the airflow, we draw on the surface, creating a pattern. Do not move your hand straight ahead, but make a curved line, thus creating a more interesting drawing.

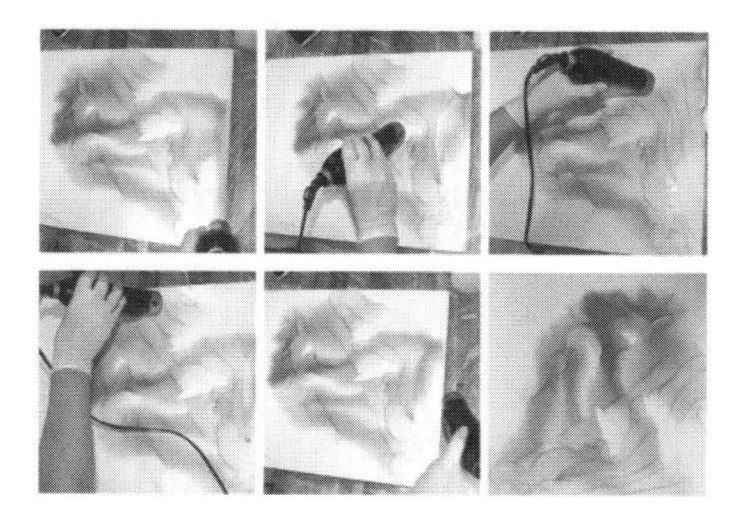

To finish the drawing, blot the excess ink and alcohol with a napkin so we won't have a dark, oily spot at the end of the drawing.

Remove the excess from the surface, giving the work a finished look. We can rasterize the work, select an individual element, cut it out, design it, or leave it as is.

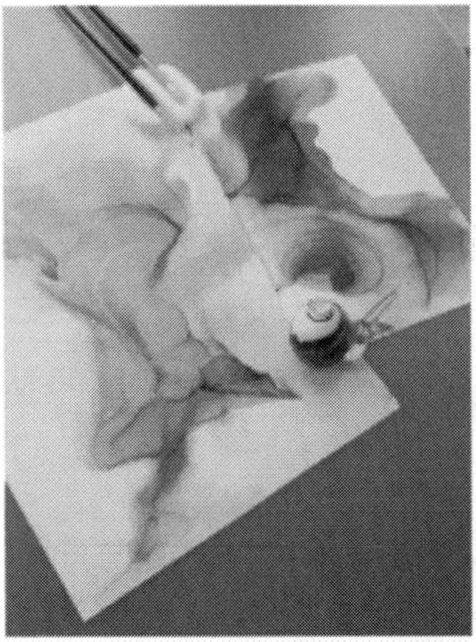
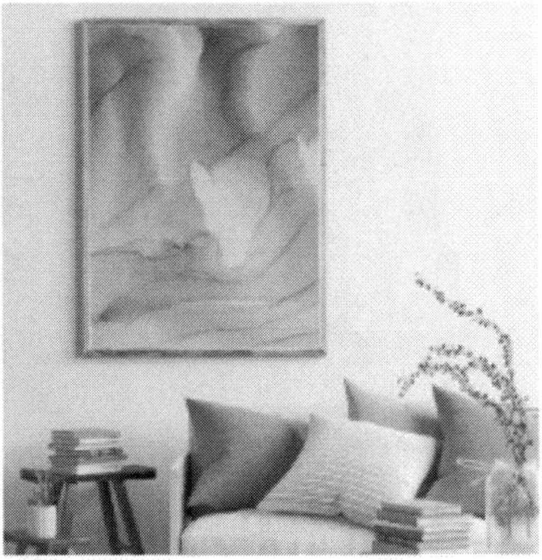
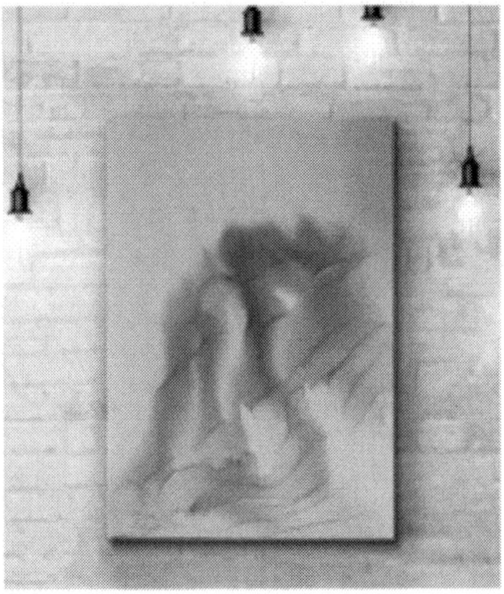
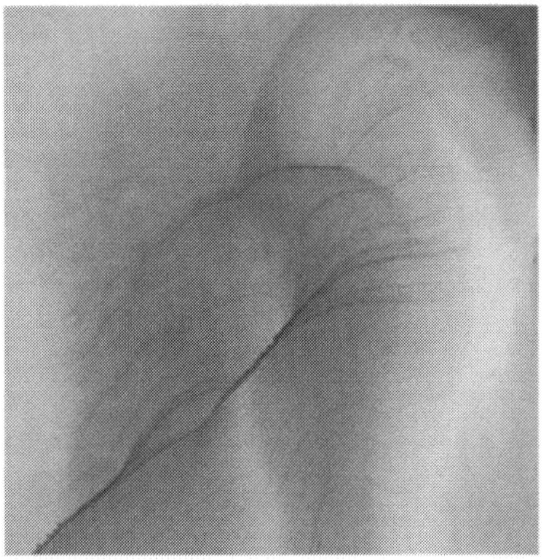

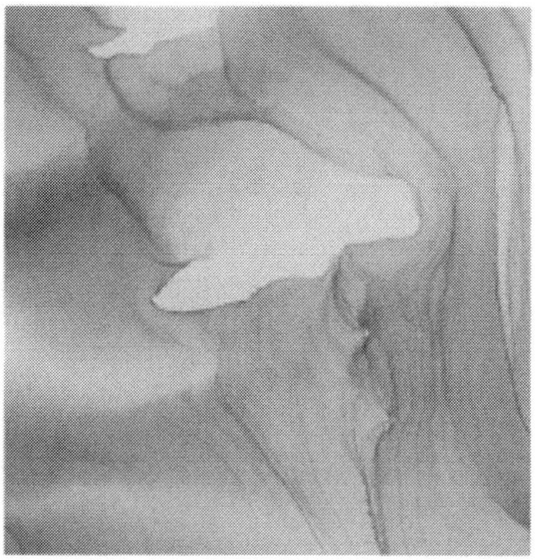

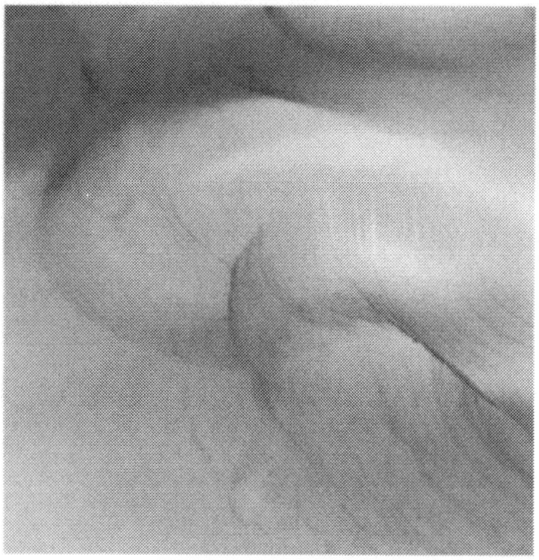

Lesson 9: Drawing Flowers with the Compressor

We will need synthetic paper, alcohol ink, Rainger "White" alcohol ink, a hairdryer, a compressor, a white pen or Posca marker, a black marker with a thin tip (0.2), and isopropyl alcohol in a small container with a tip.

As I do. Example:

First option:
I wipe the surface with alcohol to remove dust. I create a splatter background with a sprayer containing ink diluted in alcohol.
Then just above the center of the surface, I apply the first drop of wine-colored ink (Copic R59). In the second drop, I add the first wine color (Copic R59). The second and third drops are made with the ink of another color - turquoise (Copic B24).

The first drop should be more extensive in area than the other two. I dry these stains with a hairdryer to stay in place without splashing them.

I gently drip alcohol and use a compressor to distribute the ink on the first dried ink spot on the side until it dries. Your hand should be tilted so that your petal spreads smoothly and beautifully over the surface.

I gently drop the second drop of alcohol next to the first petal and distribute the stain with the compressor. These two colors give a deep, dark wine color when mixed.

Do this many times to get a pattern that looks like a fancy flower.

Next, take a water brush with alcohol. Use this brush to draw the sepals from the base of the flower. Use the white Posca marker to create light on the petals. You will get a 3D effect.

The big spot on top will look like the ovary of a flower. Apply black ink dots with a brush all over the ovary. Your fancy flower created with the compressor is ready.

COPIC "CARDINAL" R59
COPIC "SKY" B24

110

The second option:

We make a flower similar to the first option, but there are some differences.

In the center of a sheet of synthetic paper, I put 4 drops of Copic R24 ink. Then I add one drop of Pinata "Bronza" ink in the center of the color spot.

I dry these spots with a hairdryer to stay in place without splashing them.

I carefully add alcohol (2 drops) to the dried ink stain and use a compressor to distribute the ink and alcohol until it dries. My hand should be tilted so that our petals will spread smoothly and beautifully over the surface. I add 1-2 drops of alcohol next to this petal and distribute the ink spot with the compressor.

You should have a finished first layer of the flower. In the middle of the flower, I add another contrasting color of ink (3-4 drops). I have Pinata "Violett." I dry the center of the flower with a hairdryer.

Next, I repeat the steps in creating the first layer of the flower. I pour alcohol and blow with a compressor. Finish the leaves with the compressor to the middle of the flower. When mixing the ink, I get a different beautiful color.

I have a void in the center because the color is distributed on the leaves, and to make the image look like a flower, I put ink in the very center of the flower with a brush. Then I create volume and light with a white marker.

Our flower is ready! We protect our work from the sun and fade it with acrylic varnish. Then I use green ink and a thin brush to finish the flower.

Lesson 10: The "Rose Handle " technique.

Our task is to learn how to create roses in ink. You can create these flowers in different ways, and I'll show you some examples.

How I do it. Example:

First way:

I prepare a bottle with alcohol and ink in advance. I add the ink (Pinata "Magenta") to the bottle more petite than the alcohol.

I drop three drops of diluted ink on a synthetic surface and add more pure alcohol around this color spot. I begin to fan the ink stain to have a base for the flower.

The size of the flower base depends on the desired size of the flower itself. Try to dry the ink so that there is not too much sticky layer in the center of the flower.

I then drop pure alcohol in the form of a strip into the center of the flower and start blowing so that the edge of the rose (this will be the rose) is rounded.

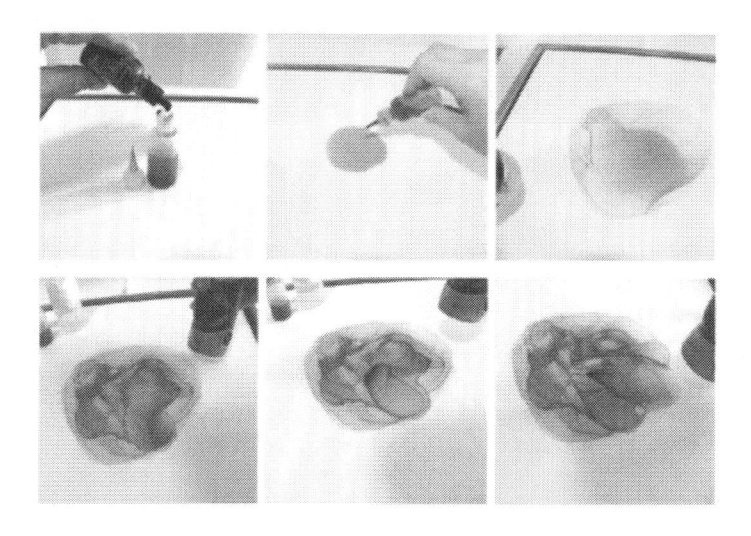

I spread the ink back and forth, making the edge of the flower soft.

In this way, I create rose petals in a circle. Again, I add ink with alcohol in a semi-circle in the center, then distribute it with a hairdryer on low speed. I try to finish drying the ink in the center so I can use the same ink again.

I don't dry the ink stain to the end because it will be more challenging to distribute.

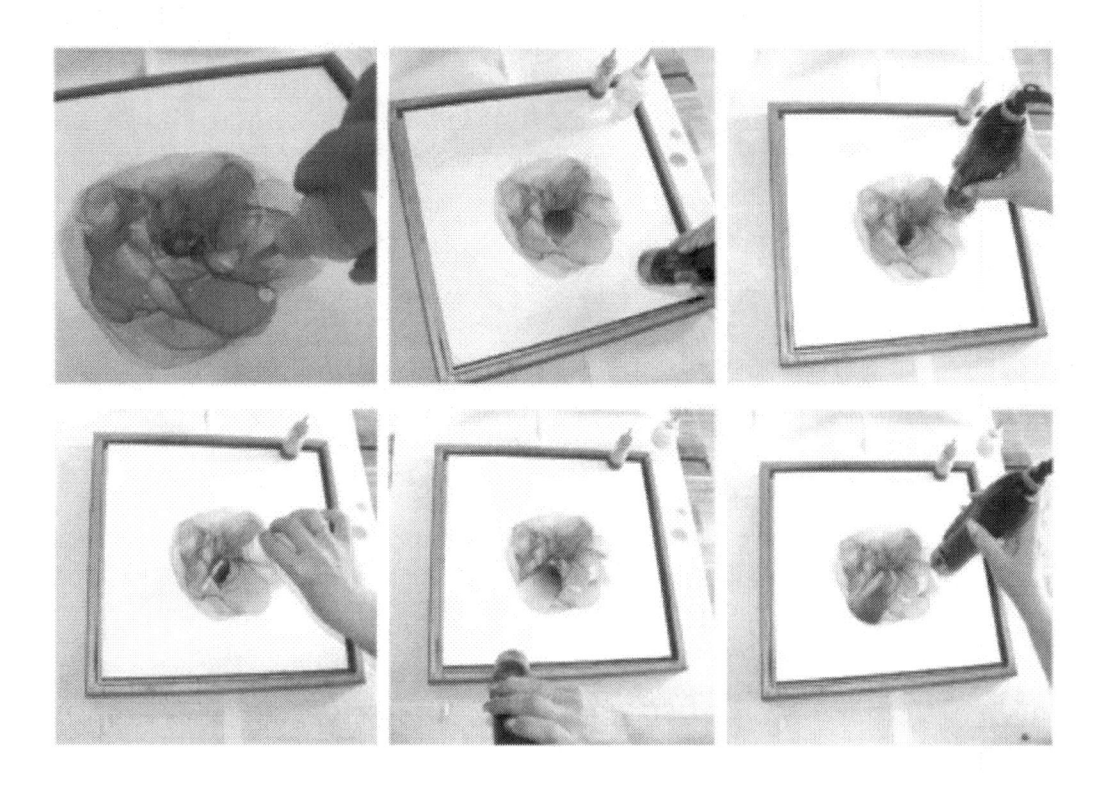

Next is the layering of petals. The edges of the flower should be soft, without worms. Petals should be layered in circles. With each circle, my petals get smaller and smaller in size.

Blot the excess ink in the center of the flower with paper.

I keep making the same moves: adding alcohol, making the petals smaller and smaller, and moving toward the center.

You can practice and create, for example, a multicolor rose from two colors of ink. A brush dipped slightly in alcohol can be used to dot so that we have a finished rose look. I made a splash effect of green all over the surface and drew more roses around the central flower.

Second method:
I start with a puddle of isopropyl alcohol in the center of the sheet surface and add two drops of Copic "Blue" B97 ink. Then I roll out the ink to spread out in a circle. I roll it out without using a hairdryer by tilting the paper in different directions.

I additionally add three drops of alcohol to the rolled-out ink.
Next, I distribute the ink spot evenly with a stream of air on all sides, creating uneven lines. I blow a straight stream of air into the ink puddle. This way, the flower will have a more realistic look.

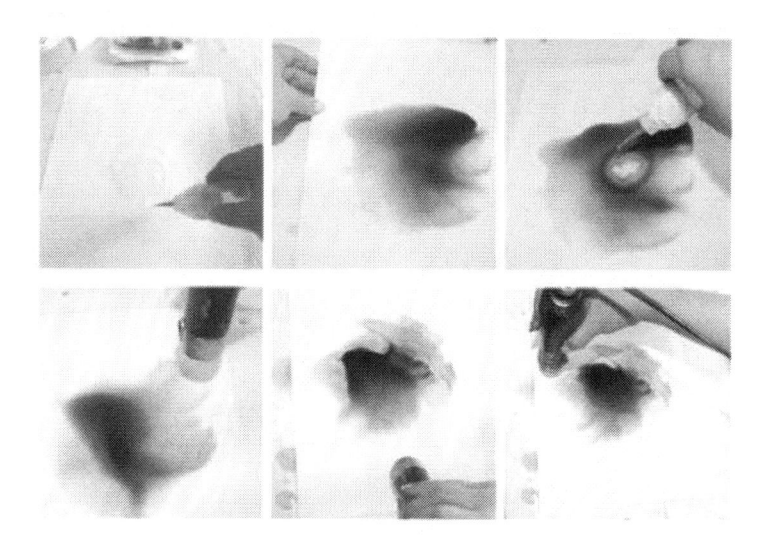

When the ink stain on the sides is a little dry, I continue to run the hairdryer on low speed in a circle. Keep the hairdryer just above the surface, further away from the ink spot. It would help if you got the soft edges of the rose.

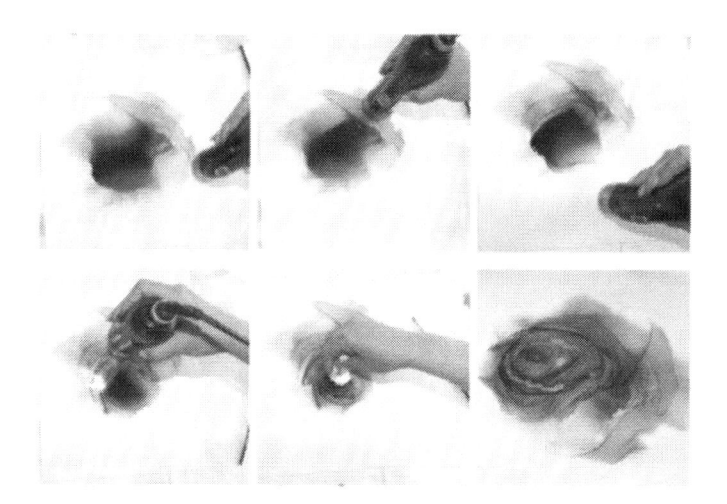

I continue to run the hairdryer in a circular motion to the end (to the middle of the flower).

If desired, you can add alcohol and dry the ink to the middle of the flower again.

If necessary, blot excess ink with a napkin.

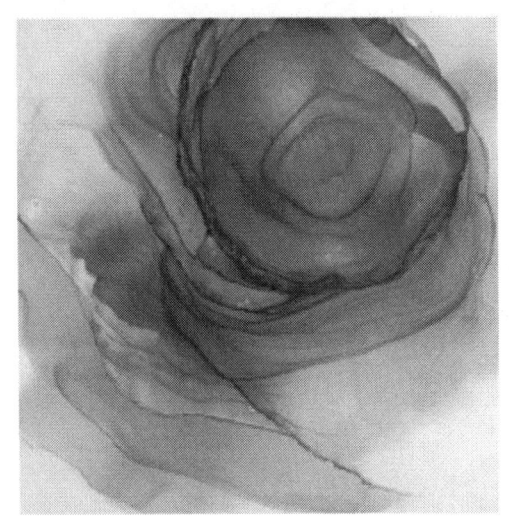

There are many ways to create roses; use your imagination, and you will succeed!

Lesson 11: Creating Rings in Ink

You will need synthetic paper, a mask, gloves, masking tape, ink, alcohol, a hairdryer, a bottle with a needle tip, and any round shapes (plastic, iron cups, jars, lids).

How I do it. Example:

First option:
Attach the synthetic paper with painter's tape to the work surface. Sketch in advance how the circles will be arranged on the paper, using the composition rule. Using the rule of thirds, I accentuate my circles to fall on the focal points (see chapter 10 for more on this).

I place the first round form (glass) on the surface. I carefully pour the alcohol around it and then the Copic "Garnet" R039 ink. If you want a darker color, don't use alcohol; just pour the ink around the mold.

I dry the ink with a hairdryer until it is scorched. I dry the ink in a circular motion on a low setting.

I control the ink with the hairdryer so the circle doesn't spread or get wide.

For the other circles, I use a different ink - Ranger Citrus. And in the same way, I dry them with a hairdryer.

❖ *Be careful when choosing colors. Try the ink on a separate sheet first, and see how it will color when mixed. Remember: the ink will mix to form a new color.*

Then I drop a small amount (1-2 drops) of isopropyl alcohol on the outside edge of the circle. I use a compressor to create a haze effect around the edges, blowing alcohol from the circle and then back again.

Add a small amount of iso in the direction you want to direct the color patches. Direct the airflow to the outer edge and back if you want the edges to be lighter. Repeat the process.

I use an alcohol atomizer to create a splatter effect. Instead of pure alcohol, you can add undiluted ink of different colors.

After dealing with the circles, I pour some alcohol (2 drops) into the palette and mix it with the Ranger Citrus ink. Then I use a brush to make the fancy droplets.

When the work is done, I remove the tape. Any painting can be rasterized and converted to the desired version by zooming in or out. I trim the picture to the desired effect. I choose the most extensive circle as the accent. I like the haze effect around it.

Second option:

I put Copic "Blue-Green" BG09 ink on the synthetic paper in a chaotic pattern and pour alcohol around the ink.

I spread the ink with a stream of air (hair dryer on speed one) over the entire area, creating a beautiful shape. Then I dry it slowly, without giving any direction to the pattern. My goal is for the edges to be airy, not stiff.

Applying the rule of thirds, I accentuate my circles to fall on the focal points. Around each shape, I pour ink and alcohol.

I start to distribute the ink over the entire area with a hairdryer at low speed, as if driving it outside the circles, working with the hairdryer at an angle.

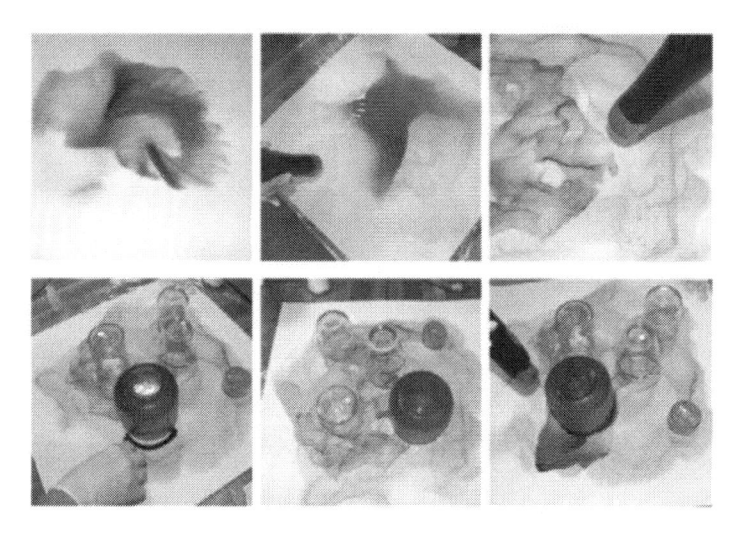

I use an alcohol sprayer to create a splatter effect. Then I use a brush to make fancy droplets with another ink color.

Next, I ink the silver from Molotow Liquid chrome.

COPIC -BLUE GREEN- BG 09

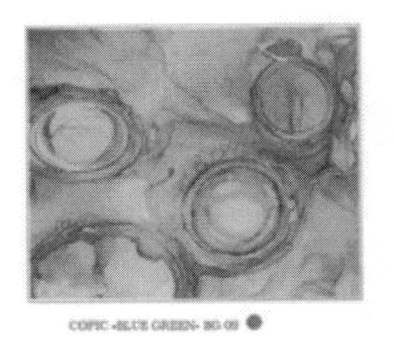

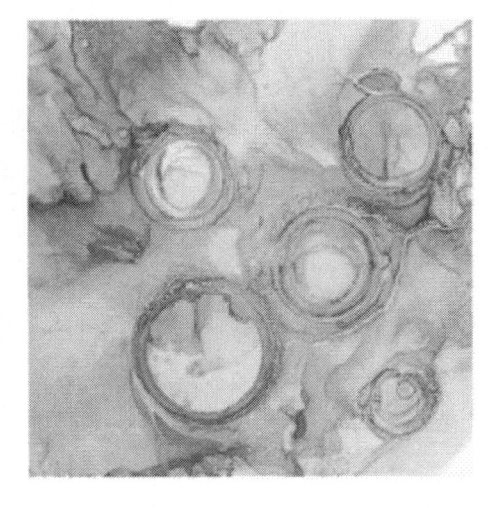

126

Lesson 12: The feathering technique

This technique aims to draw with alcohol ink on a synthetic surface in the form of feathers.

How I do it. Example:

I add ink to the surface in a small oblong drop, then add alcohol to one side.

At low speed with the airflow, I start moving this elongated drop back and forth. I tilt the paper with my other hand so that the ink drips toward the hairdryer.

I slowly blow out the color spot with a hairdryer in a semicircular motion at low speed, from top to bottom. I tilt the paper so that the ink spot moves in the direction I want.

Adding more ink will require more alcohol. To ensure the feathers don't have clear borders, I add alcohol to the feather's edge and continue working without stopping.

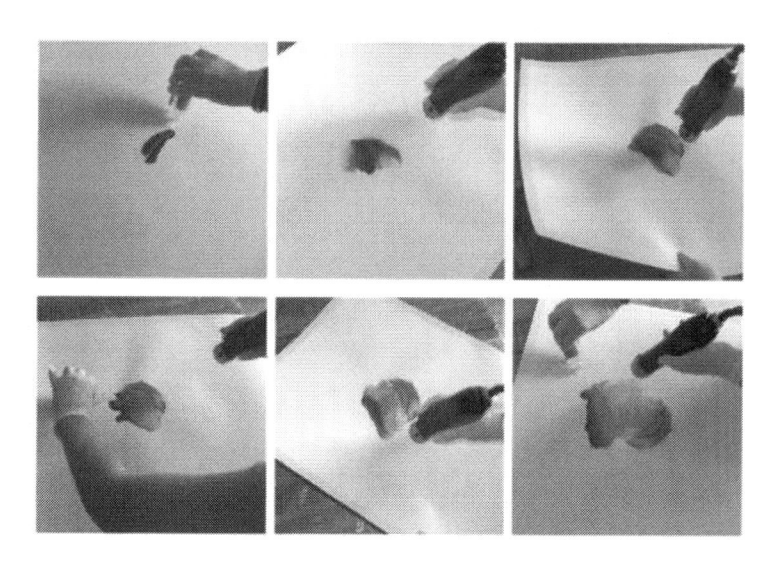

Finish the elements to the end; otherwise, there may be oily torn edges. If necessary, gently blot the excess ink with the tip of a napkin and continue drying to the end.

My task is to paint the feathers in monochrome, applying a degree of saturation from dark to light and diluting the iso shades with alcohol.

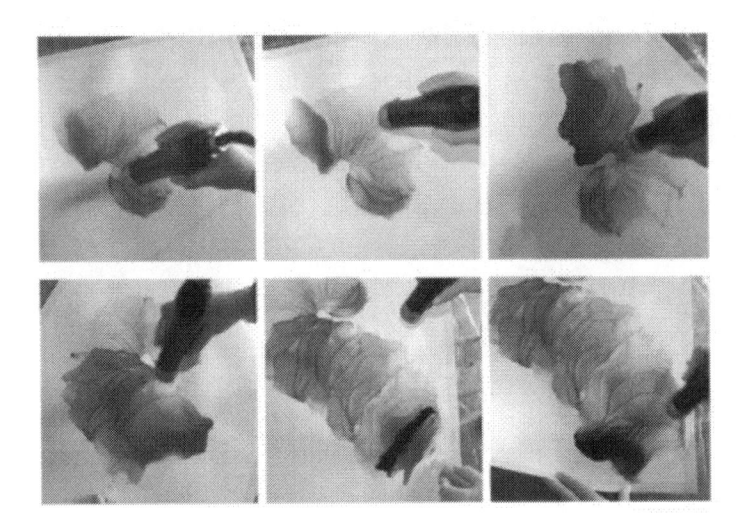

I continue to hold the hairdryer perpendicular to the surface, running the ink spot over the in a semi-circle, swirling it inward, turning the surface.

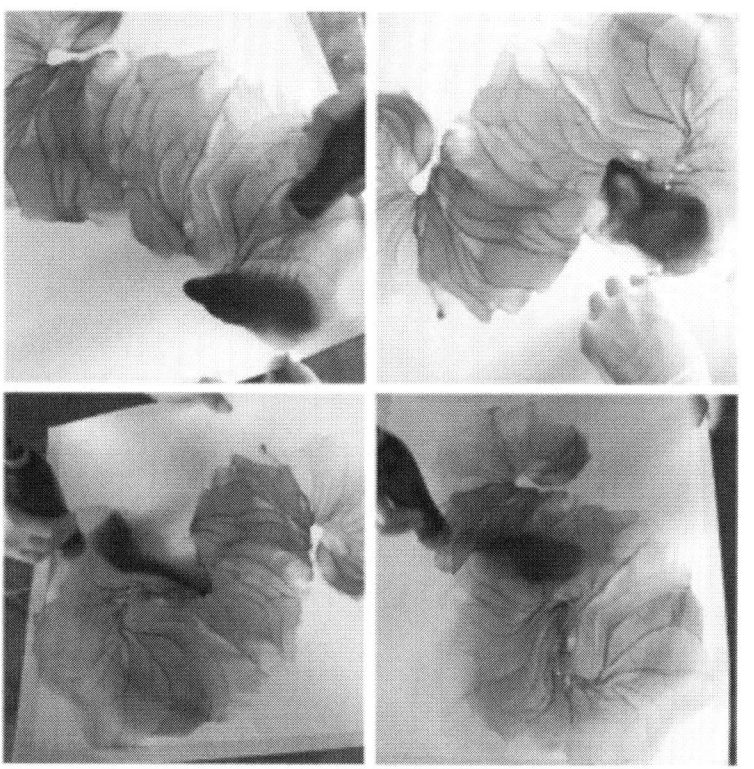

I constantly make the same motion: I add alcohol to the entire surface of the feather, blurring the precise boundaries.

When I finish the feathering, I dry the ink spot in the center in an encompassing circular motion, moving toward the center of the work.

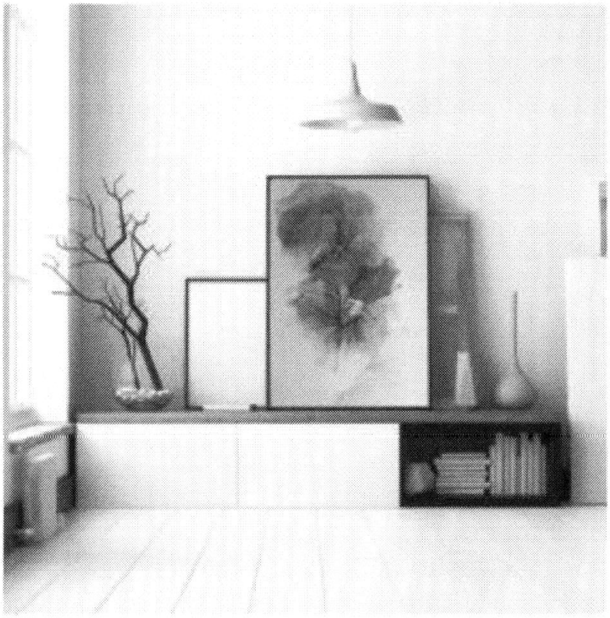

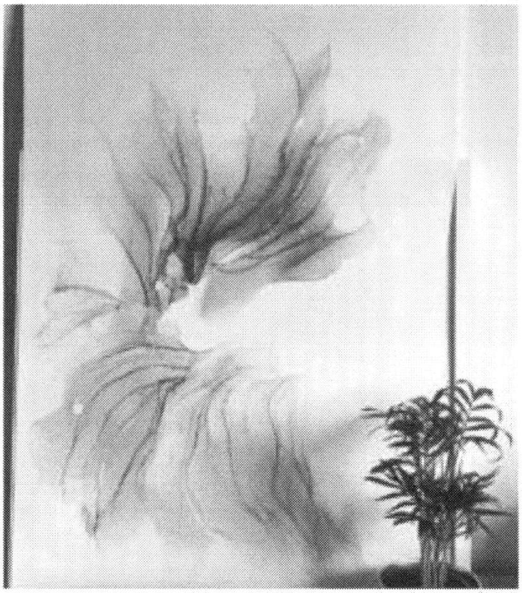

Lesson 13: Plot works

Alcohol ink can also draw subject matter: flowers, landscapes, mountains, cacti, flora, and fauna. For example, the "flush" method is used when creating landscapes, with the paper tilted so that the ink flows in the right direction. Then details are drawn: trees, houses, people, etc.

How I do it. Example:

Flowers:
I create a multi-layered flower with a low-power hairdryer.

I apply undiluted ink of two colors (Copic "Carnet" R39 and Ranger "Ametist") to the surface in a circle, alternating spots of one and another color - as shown in the photo. I dry the ink a little so that it does not drip.

I add a little alcohol and start drying at the base of the flower. I run a stream of air up and down to get a soft stretch of color. This will be the first petal. I collect the remaining ink at the end of the petal with a napkin and finish drying the petal.

Next to the first petal, I add a drop of ink and alcohol and start drying with a hairdryer in the same way - taking the petal down on one side. Using a brush, I attach it to the next petal of the flower. I blot the rest of the ink at the bottom of the petal with a napkin.

❖ *Shape the petals in a circle. Don't run the hairdryer from different sides! Hold the hairdryer on one side, toward the bottom, toward the base of the flower. To keep the ink from escaping, bend the paper in different directions.*

I place the following petals in the foreground, creating a volume effect. It turns out that the petal in the foreground can overlap the back. I build up the petals, layering them on top of each other. I use a brush to outline the petals. I create petals arranged in a circle with a drop of alcohol and a stream of air.

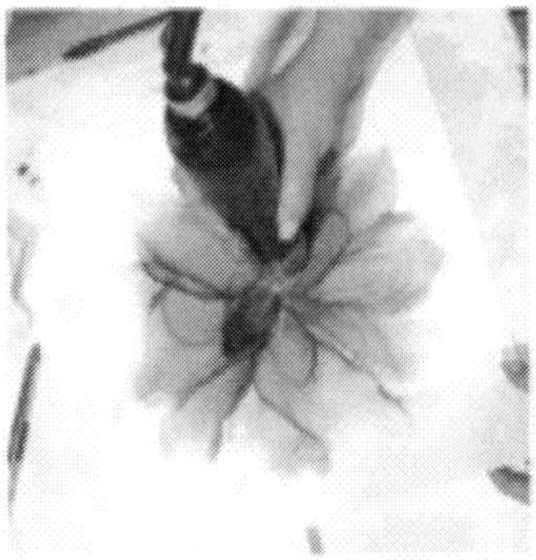
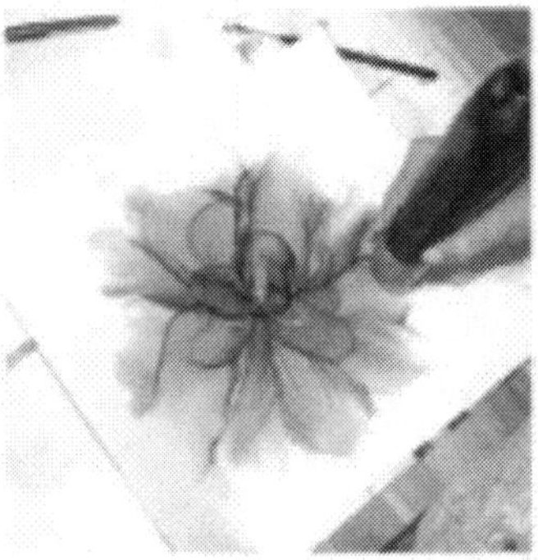
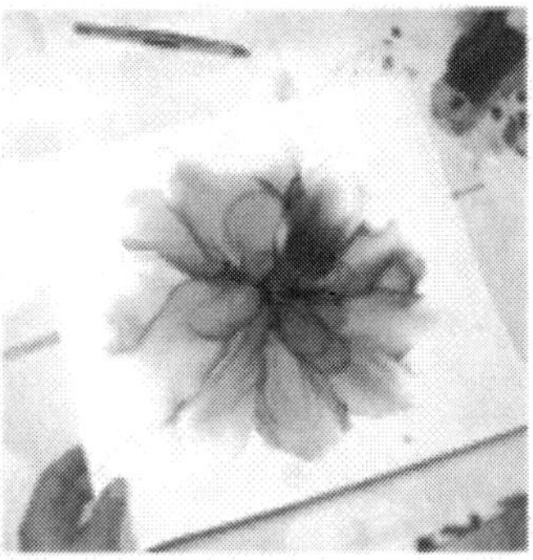
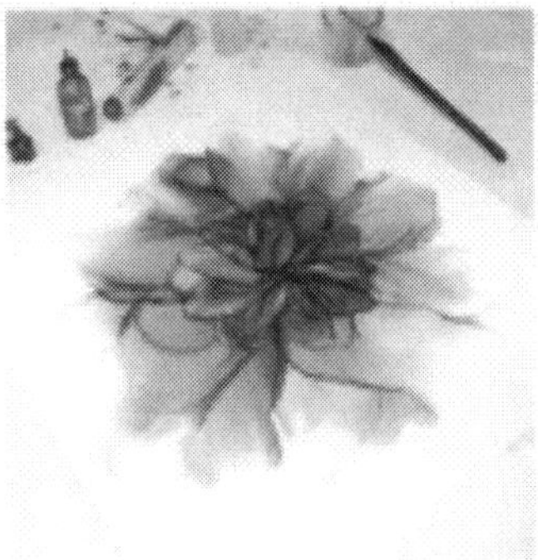
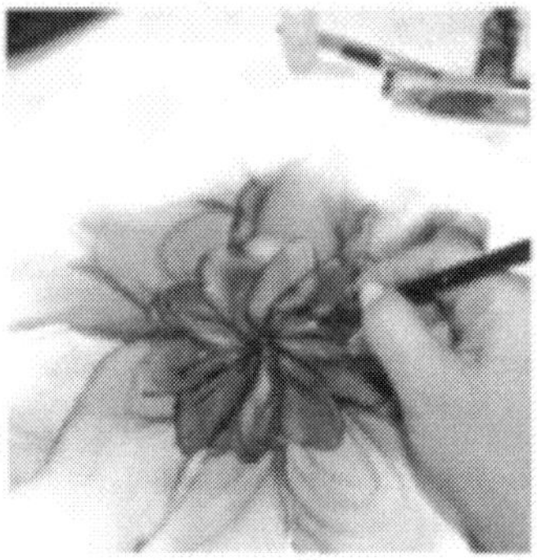
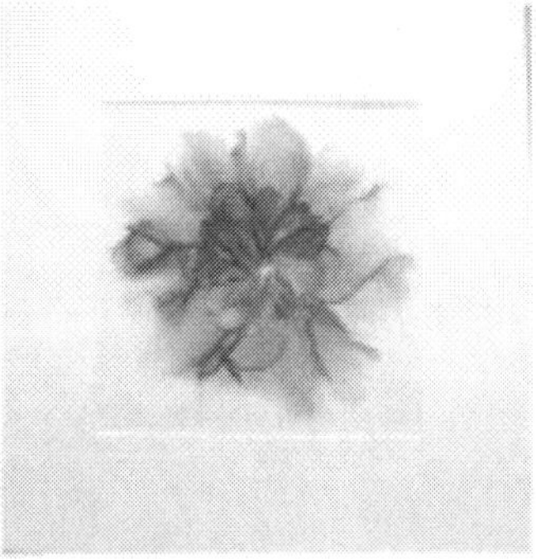
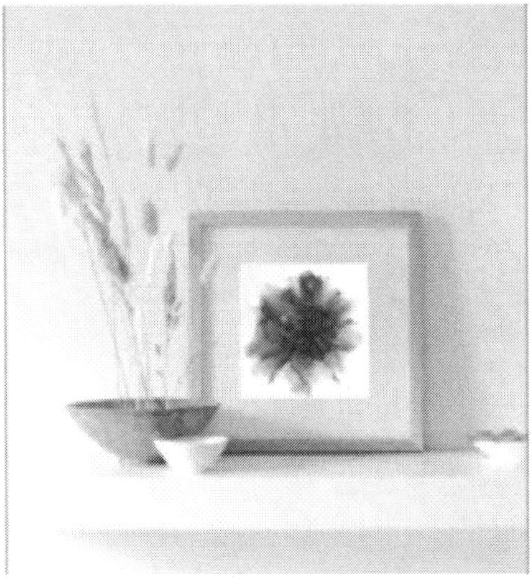

Animals:

I start the work with the preparatory stage - with the background. I do the work with a brush - a fan over the entire surface - from top to bottom.

I distribute ink in strips of different colors. The strips lay down beautifully, and the process can be repeated if necessary. Then, I distribute a little alcohol in strips in the same way.

Then, I outline the drawing using a brush with a reservoir filled with alcohol.

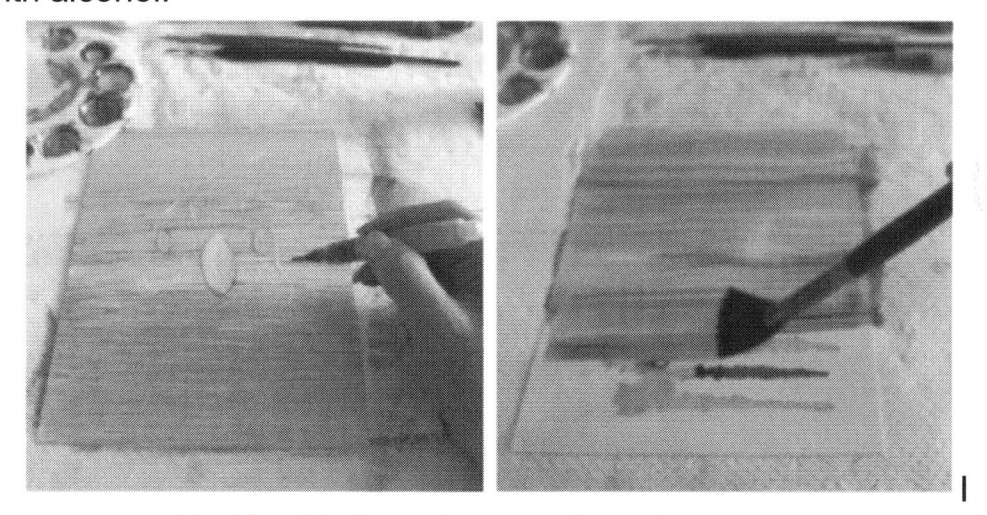

I then proceed to identify the primary color schemes.

❖ *Mix the ink on the palette, and find the shades you like. It all depends on your color preferences.*

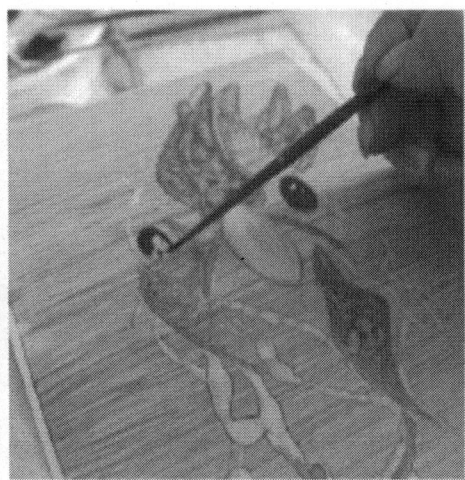

I start by working out the highlights throughout the picture. Then I move on to the drawing of halftones. I avoid excessive amounts of ink so there is no "dirt." Then I work piece by piece, working through the details, element by element.

I apply alcohol ink with a spot effect on the surface, using a minimal amount of isopropyl alcohol.

❖ *Keep in mind that the ink applied continues to move until it dries. More ink control can be achieved by applying minimal or no alcohol to certain areas.*

I apply the ink to the desired 1mm line. For faster drying of the ink, you can blow on it.

I use a thin brush and wand to create contrast between the individual elements, which are the accent of the image. A small amount of alcohol on the wand with alcohol on the drawing leaves gaps - this gives an additional exciting texture to the image of the rooster.

With a brush soaked in alcohol, I add or remove unnecessary strokes until I am satisfied with the work's depth and volume. The main thing is to stop in time.

People:

I start with the background. I spread a puddle of alcohol over the surface and add ink in a semi-circle. I gently add alcohol in a circle and start blowing with a hairdryer at low speed.

I lead the airflow in a semi-circle of color (ink) stain to the bottom.

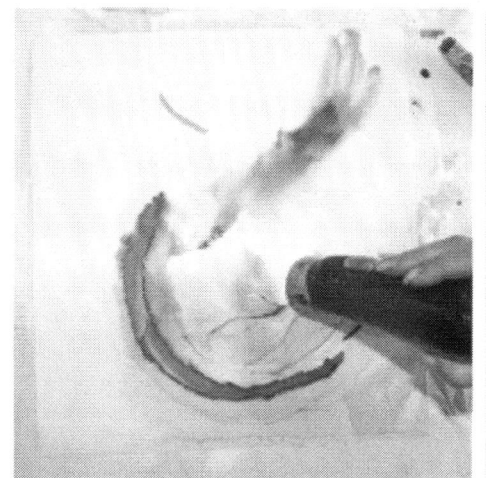

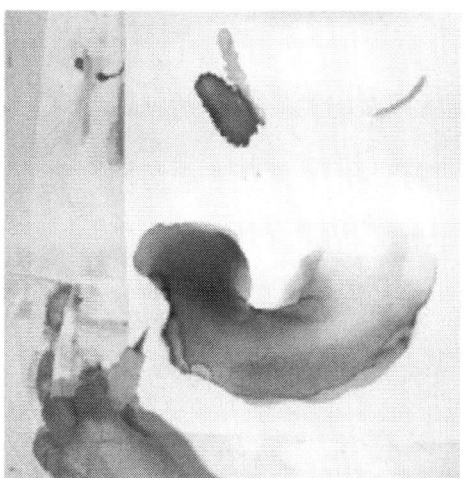

To make the entry soft, you need to dry the paint, starting from the edge of the work and towards the center.

Next comes the incorporation of the girl into the drawing and drawing details.

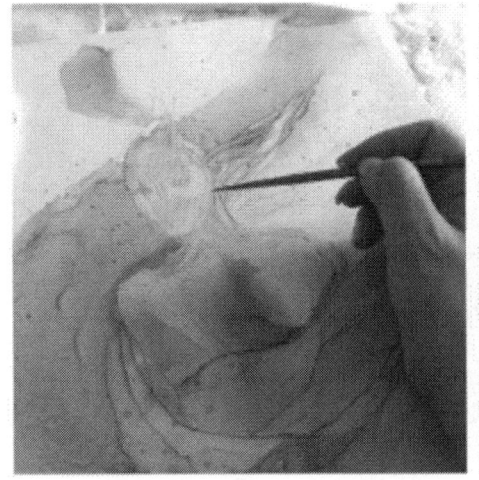

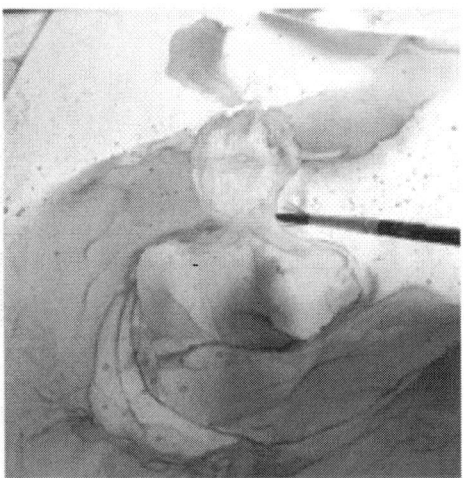

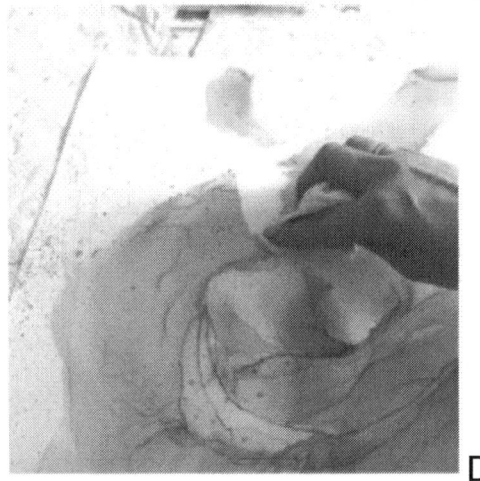

Drawing the details of the body is not easy. I gently erase part of the drawing for the girl's figure with alcohol, using watercolor painting techniques. The ink can be applied in strokes, dots, and lines, using a small amount of alcohol with a hairdryer. Different brushes can change the shape of strokes or dots, change the angle, and reduce or increase the pressure on the brush.

The lower the ink concentration, the weaker the tint.
With a fine-tipped brush, I draw the dark areas of the girl's silhouette with undiluted ink, and then with an alcohol brush without

ink, I retouch the precise boundaries of these dark areas.

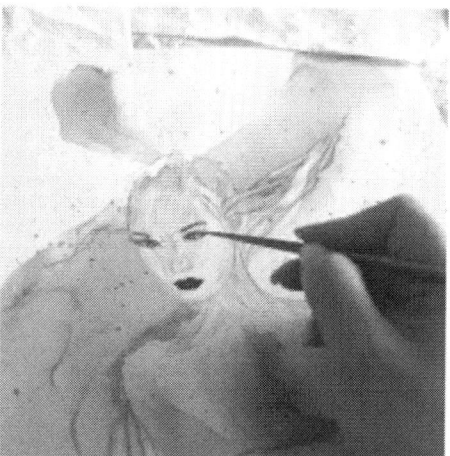

Lesson 14: Applying Alcohol Painting with the Pebeo Contour

You will need a laminated surface, stamp pad, alcohol ink in different colors, a fine brush, the palette for color dilution, isopropyl alcohol, outline, and firm Pebeo.

As I do. Example:

I first apply Ranger "Slate" ink with an alcohol stamp pad to the surface and create a general color background on the surface.

I lighten the center of the surface a little bit with alcohol. After that, I draw with a pencil.

Then I use the Pebeo outline to trace all of the borders of the drawing. It turns out that the outline separates the gaps between the colors, and the colors of the alcohol ink are preserved without blurring or overlapping each other.

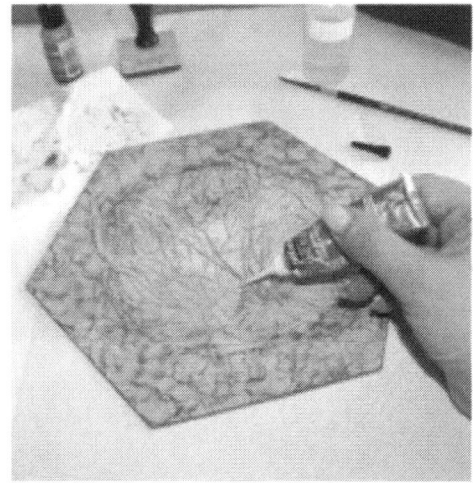

I wait until the outline dries. It took me about 15 minutes. Then I start painting each sector in its color with ink.

I mix the ink with alcohol to get a tone, look for the right tone, and apply it to the surface.

If I need a darker color, I use ink without alcohol; if I need a lighter color, I stir in a palette of the base color and add a drop of alcohol.

In this way, I put all the paints on the surface.

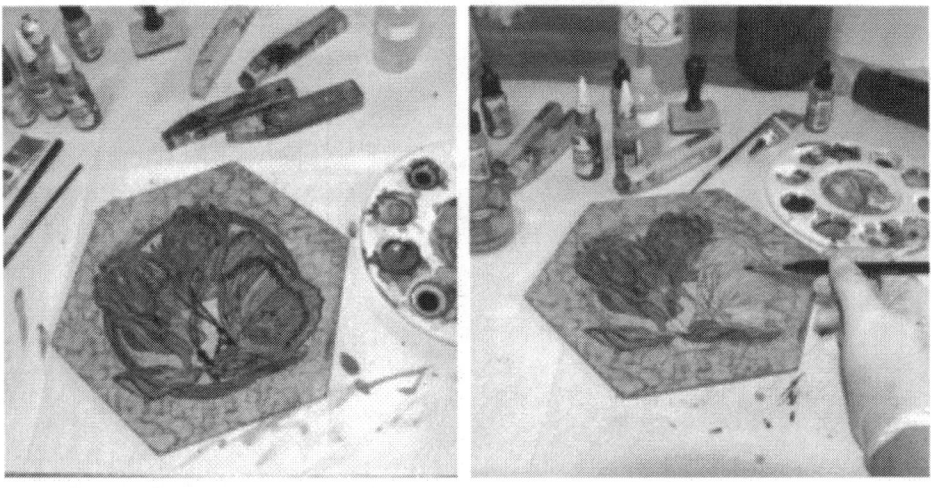

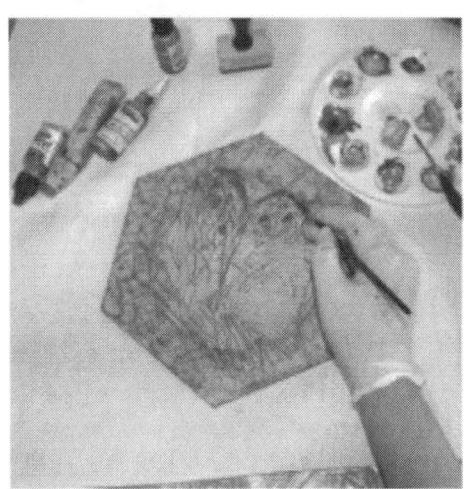

The edges of the surface can be gilded with liquid gilding or framed.

You can use the outline and resin to make beautiful gift holders, candle holders, and large paintings (and maybe even on canvas - why not?).

Don't be afraid to experiment because many exciting ideas lurk behind experiments.

Lesson 15: Decorating paintings with additional tools and materials

After painting a picture with alcoholic ink, you can decorate your work with different materials, which are sure to add their accent to your work.

How I do it. Example:

1. **Brighten the painting with the help of sheet metal.** In some places, lighten the picture with foil sheet gilding. At work, you can use both liquid gilding and flakes. In the beginning, I create the picture. I trace a circle in the accessible areas.

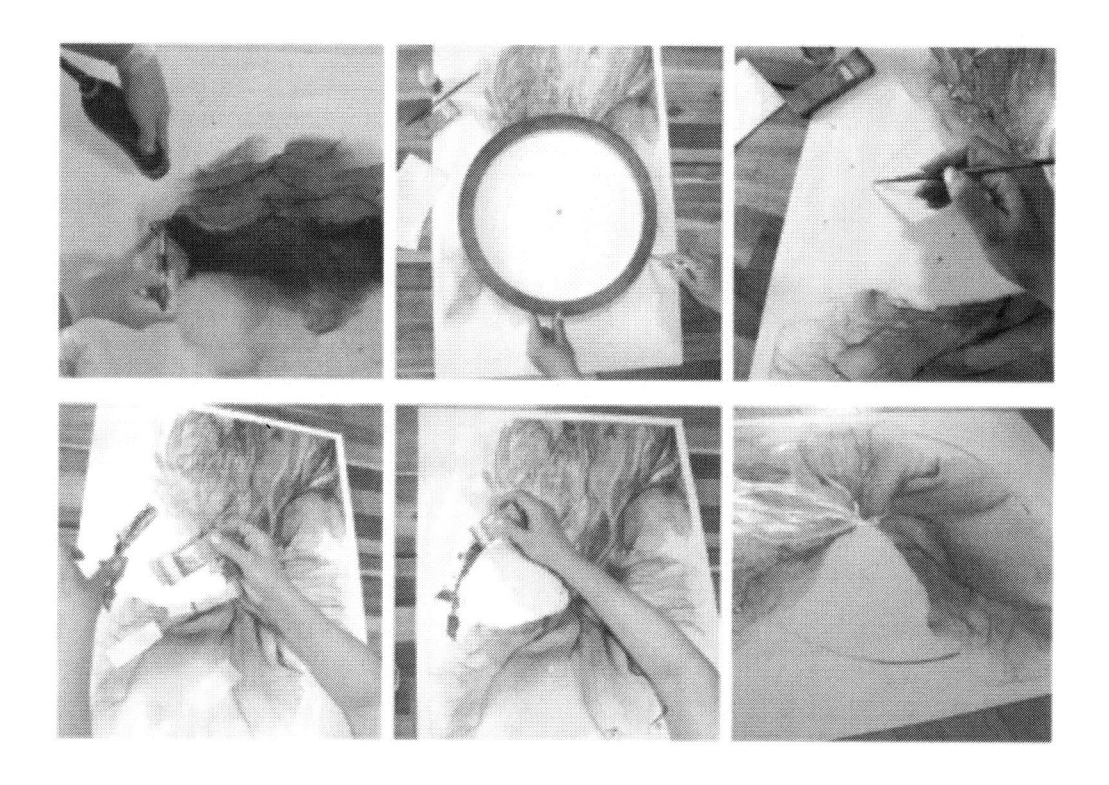

To cover the picture with the sheeting, draw a strip with a thin brush with the gauze glue. Please wait for it to dry for 1 minute (the time varies from manufacturer to manufacturer), and then carefully apply the sheet of the tape with a dry brush and tweezers.
I press the gauze to the surface with a brush and then brush off the excess (residual gauze) with a stiff brush.

❖ *How do you know when you can glue the gilding? The spot where the glue is applied must be "dry." If the place where you applied the glue is still wet, you have to wait. Otherwise, the gilding may curl and not unfold completely, and the luster will be lost.*

2.**Using a kitchen sponge.** I put different colors on the sponge, put a little alcohol on top, and draw different winding lines on the synthetic paper. Afterward, I play with the markers a little bit. I like how beautifully Edding markers lay down. This way, I add a little bit to the image of the picture.

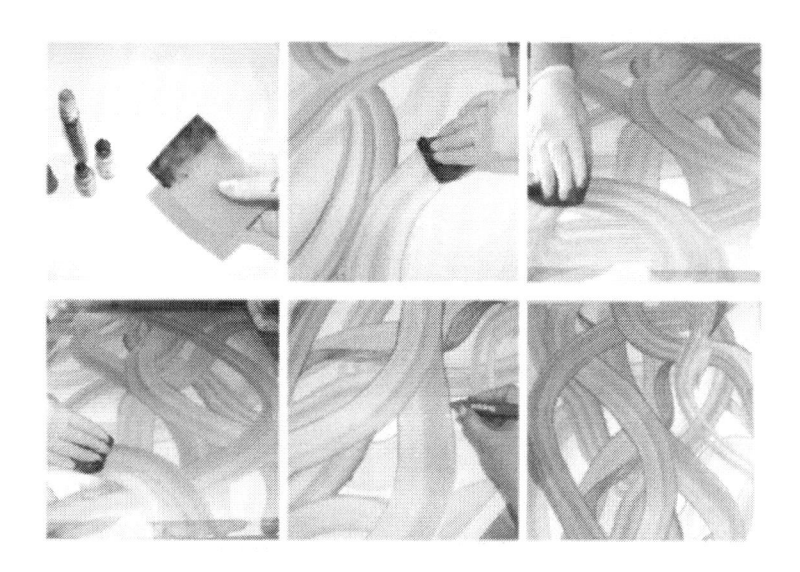

3. The air pump or blower.

This is used to blow out alcohol ink. It is sold on the expanse of AMAZON. Use the air pump to blow out the alcohol ink, repeating until you have completed your drawing.

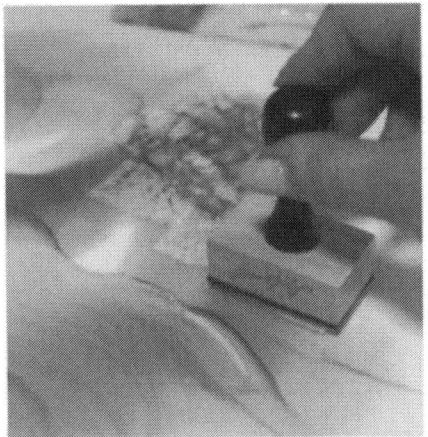

4. **Stamp pad**. With the help of white felt and a couple of drops of alcohol, this pad can make interesting strokes on your paintings.

5. **Natural motifs.** Draw with leaves. Dip the leaf into the ink. We press it to the paper's surface, dry it with a hairdryer so that the ink dries under the leaf, and then take the leaf away. This leaves a print on the paper - perfect for plant motifs.

6. **Acrylic paints.** We can apply acrylic paints to the finished background made with alcohol ink. It turns out to be an exciting combination.

Lesson 16: Géode with a brush

Jade is a natural mineral of volcanic rock. You can use alcohol ink to create an image similar to a slice of jade.

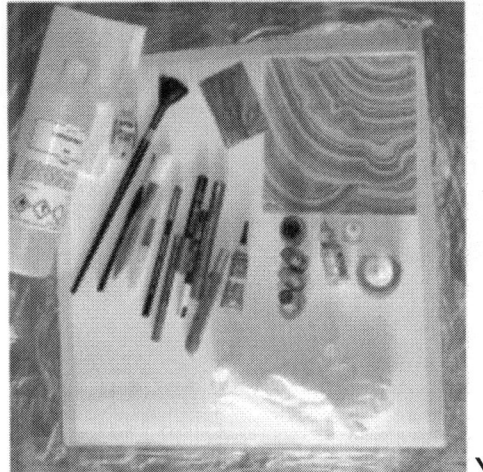

You will need: synthetic paper or laminated surface; isopropanol; brushes (fan, fine tip, broad-brush); tissues; Pebeo Vitrail glass and metal outline; posca marker (gold, white); Edding wide and thin marker; alcohol ink: Copic "Blue" B05; Copic "Blue-Green" BG09; Copic "Night Blue" B97; Tim Holtz Mixativ with Show Cap; Huids "Gold Rush."; alcohol bottle; container (this could be a palette).

How I do it. Example:

I glue construction tape around the edges.

❖ *Sketch the elaborate with the colors, so you know how your colors will be roughly arranged in advance.*

I chose a picture from the Internet as a sketch.

Using a thin brush, I draw the inner walls of the zoned layers of the geode with alcohol ink, according to the sketch. I pour Copic "Process Blue" B05 ink into an ink reservoir, about 7 to 8 drops. I add 4 drops of alcohol.

Then, I put the central contour on the surface with a broad brush.

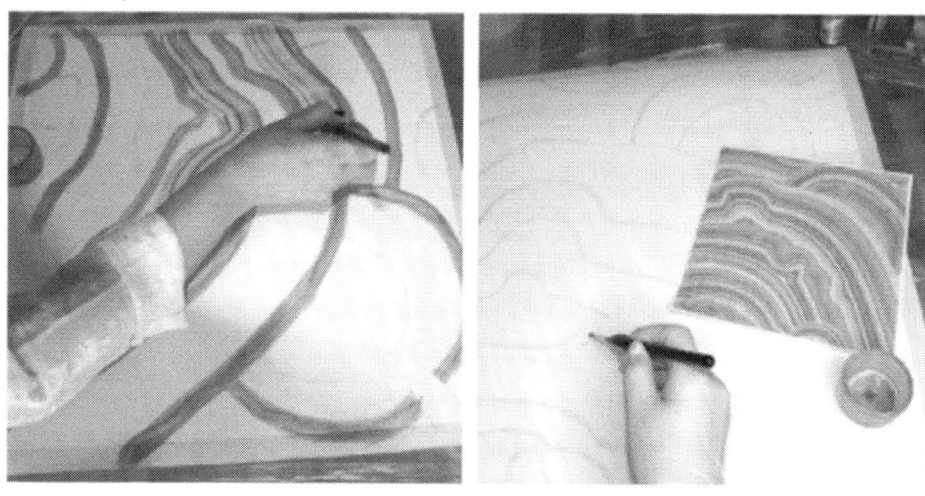

I apply to the surface where I think it is necessary. Then I take a fan brush, and from one side, add 4 drops of Copic "Night Blue" B97; from the other side, I add 4 drops of Copic "Blue-Green" BG09. The result is a beautiful gradient.

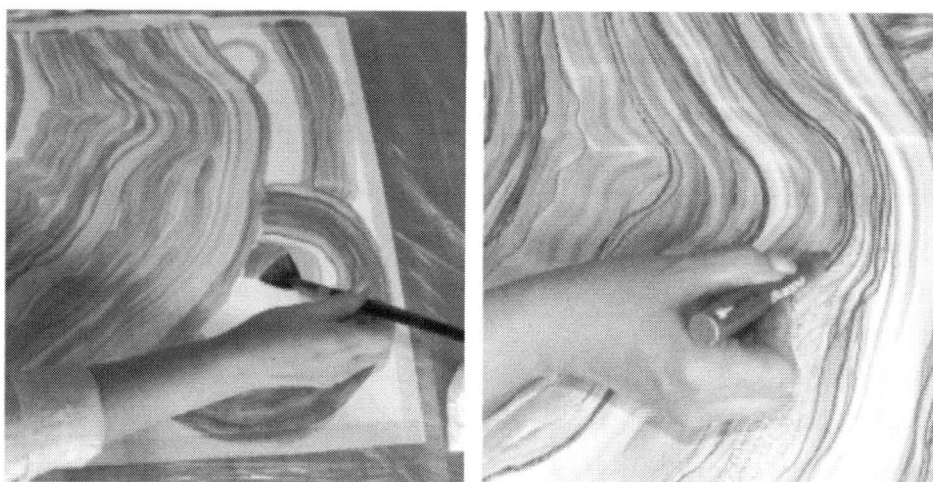

I use a broad brush soaked in alcohol to create zonal layers of jelly. I add more streaks of geode.

On top of each curve, I apply Huids "Gold Rush" metallic ink. When creating layers of a different color, I moisten the brush well in alcohol and draw the layers so that the colors do not mix. The result is beautiful veins that look like a slice of stone.

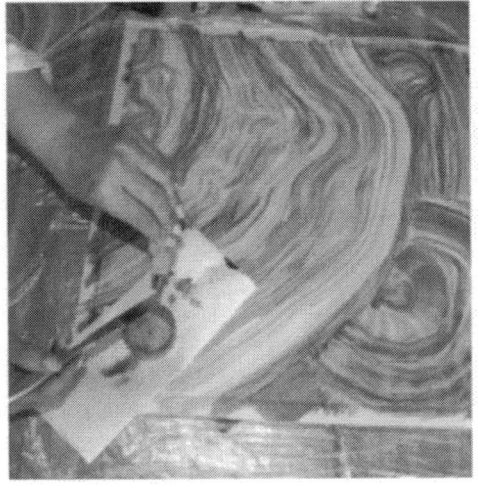

The next step is to apply lines with Pebeo Vitrail to give volume to the drawing. Then I apply another gold glitter Glitter Glue to thicker lines. The picture immediately gets a different look.

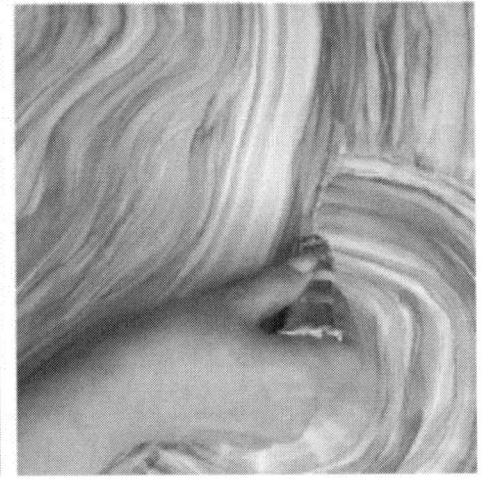

After the outlines dry, I add various details to the picture. For example, I make droplets or lines with a thin brush soaked in alcohol.

❖ *You can apply glue to one of the strips and sprinkle glitter. You can also sprinkle small pebbles on the glue to add volume and reality. It all depends on what you want!*

In the end, I carefully remove the tape all around the perimeter and wiped off the sweat with alcohol.

The final touch is to frame the picture.

Lesson 17: Soft Entries and Embedding Elements in a Painting

This lesson aims to teach how to make soft entrances into a drawing and incorporate elements into the overall composition.

A soft entry is the stretching of the ink from light to dark. The larger the surface you draw on, the easier it is to build a composition. Always have dry wipes on hand to wipe up ink leaks.

How I do it. Example:
I wipe a wooden laminated surface of 50*40 cm with alcohol. I apply the Copic "Spanish Oliva" YG97 ink on a strip on the right side. I pour alcohol around the ink.

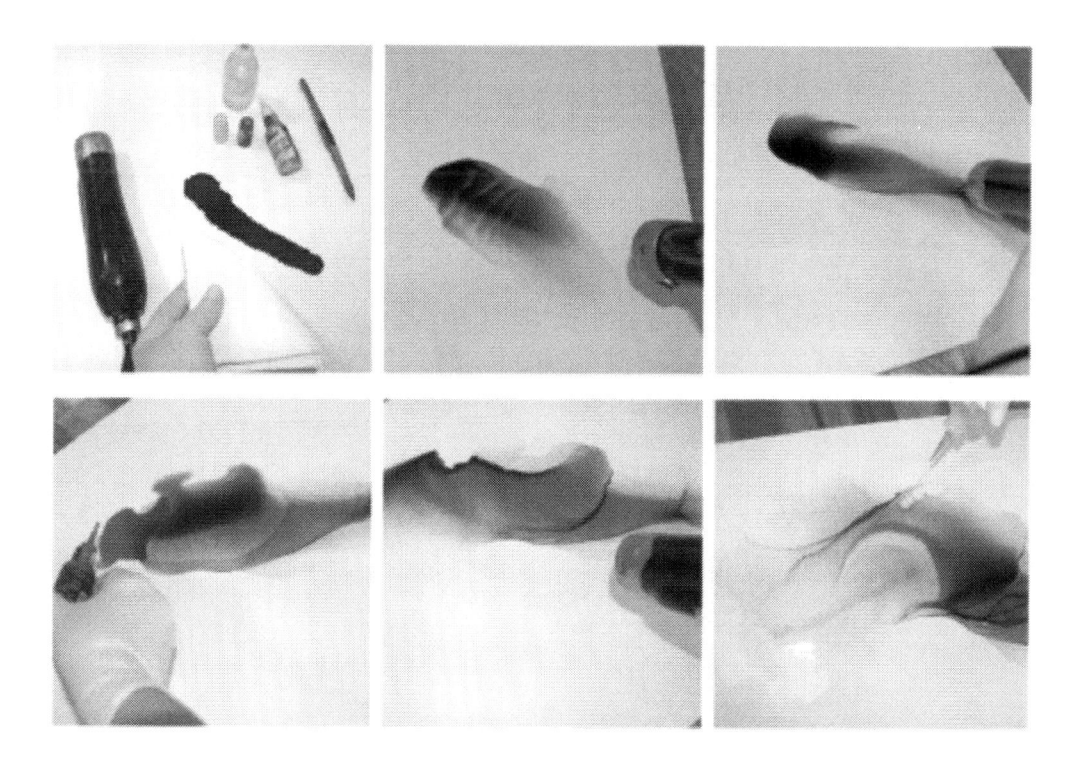

I start to move the ink spot to the center of the picture. The entry into the picture should be soft like a veil. I dry with the hairdryer at a low speed from the beginning and then move toward the center. Tilting the hairdryer tangentially, I move my first ray of air to the center.

You don't need to blow dry in a circle, and you should get a stretch of color.

I add another color of Pentart "Malow" ink and alcohol to the undried ink spot. The ink stain comes from the bottom right and is directed upward to the left. With a stream of air, I move in a circular motion from the center of the stain to let the ink open up and drive the hairdryer again to the beginning of the inlet to make it soft. I run off the ink tangentially with the hairdryer.

If I see a stiff edge, I add a little alcohol and blow that spot up again.

I make the third entry from the center by adding ink (two drops of Copic "Flash Pink" E95 and one drop of Copic "Spanish Oliva" YG97) and alcohol. I use a brush with a silicone tip to help the ink bond in the center of the design. This is how I incorporate the element into the drawing.

Using a stream of air, I gently run the ink down to the center in a circular motion. I hide all the ends in the center of the drawing. This part of the drawing is shaped like a seashell.

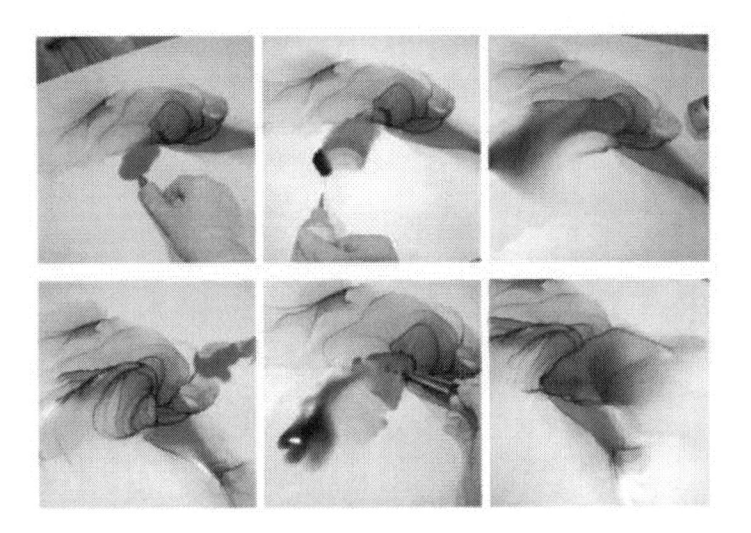

The following composition is built around the main element, which looks like a seashell. I hide the ray's end in the center, using a brush to help. I add color in places and spread it with a stream of air over the surface.

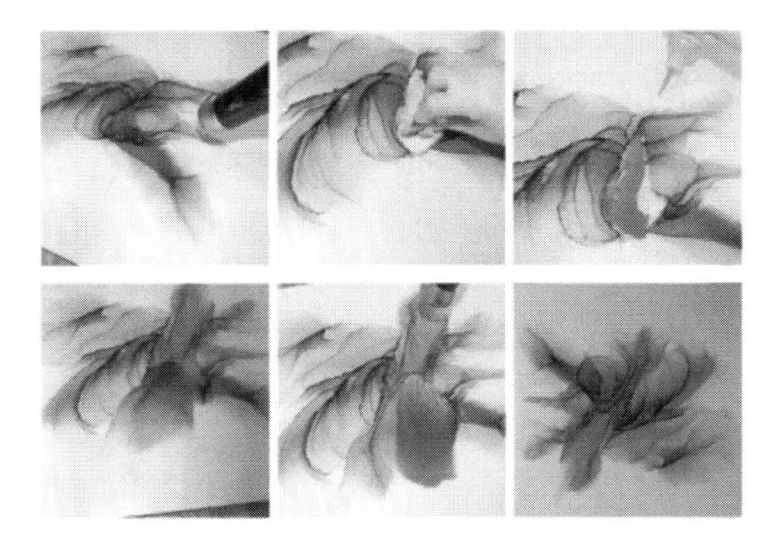

The next task is to incorporate the element into the existing pattern. To do this, I use a cloth soaked in alcohol to remove the oiliest element gently. I add ink and a little alcohol to this place. I squeeze the ink from the center of the picture to the beginning of the entrance, then vice versa, so that there are no hard edges. The airflow here is already moving tangentially, not in a circular motion.

Lesson 18: The fancy snake technique

Prepare synthetic paper, alcohol ink, alcohol, a hairdryer, a compressor, a white Posca marker, and a black marker. The petals can be created with a hairdryer, a compressor, or a blower

❖ *Determine the composition and color scheme of the picture. Consider in advance the movement of your snake. It can be a straight diagonal solution or a diagonal with a bend.*

How I do it. Example:

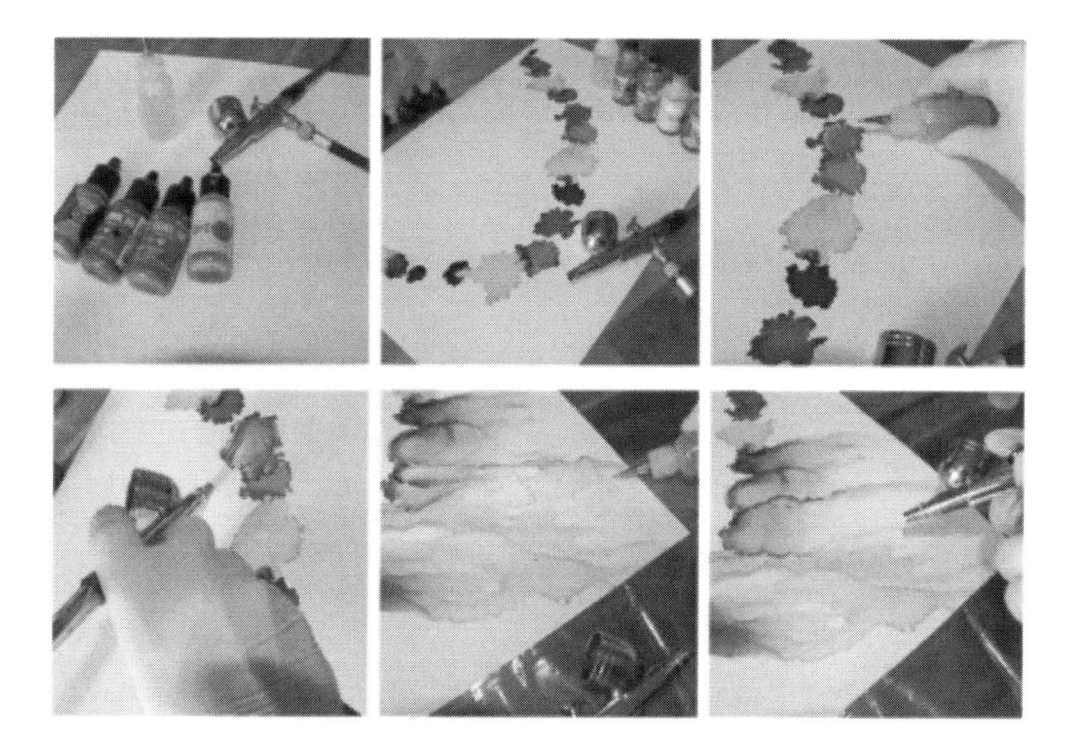

I decided to do a diagonal solution with a bend. According to the given direction of the pattern, I add one drop of ink, alternating colors: dark - light.

- ❖ Metallics (bronze, silver, gold) can be added between the drops for an accent. The drops are placed 1 cm apart so that the colors do not mix.

I wait for the drops to dry (you can hasten the drying with a hairdryer).

Near the edge of the dried ink drop, I carefully place a drop of alcohol and disperse it with a compressor (or hairdryer) at a tangential angle. The drawing will resemble the leaves of a flower.

Then I move on to another drop of dried ink and repeat the action: first, I add a drop of alcohol, then accelerate the ink and alcohol at an angle with either a blower or a compressor.

❖ *Direct the airflow to the outer edge and back if you want the edges to be lighter. Work on one side first, then work on the other.*

I clean up any leaks or ugly torn edges of the snake rays with a napkin and alcohol. Then, I draw a fancy drawing with a black marker all over the surface. You can also use a white marker.

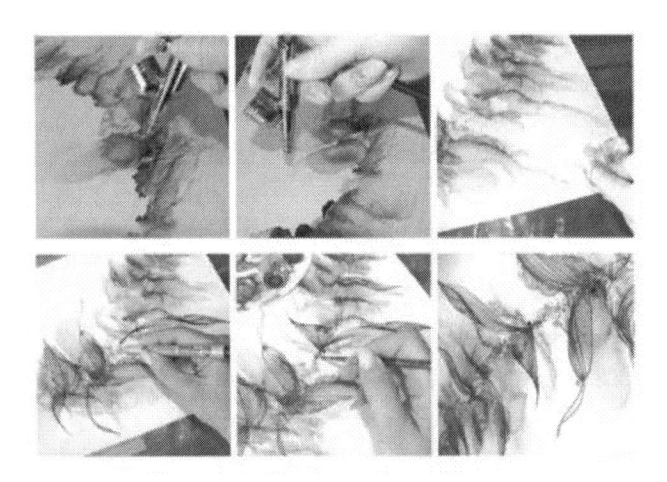

I add drops along the diagonal line. I apply them with a thin brush and alcohol. The drops are in different colors, so the effect is more interesting.

Lesson 19: Clocks with alcohol ink

In this lesson, I will show you how to draw with alcohol ink on round laminated surfaces.

How I do it. Example:

The first version of applying ink in a circle.

I apply Copic "Argyle Purple" RV99 and Copic "Light Prawn" R22 ink in a semi-circle on one part of the circle. I wipe around the laminated surface with alcohol (it can also be a clock). Then I add alcohol to the ink to open up between each other. Next, I add alcohol on the other side, so there are no hard edges.

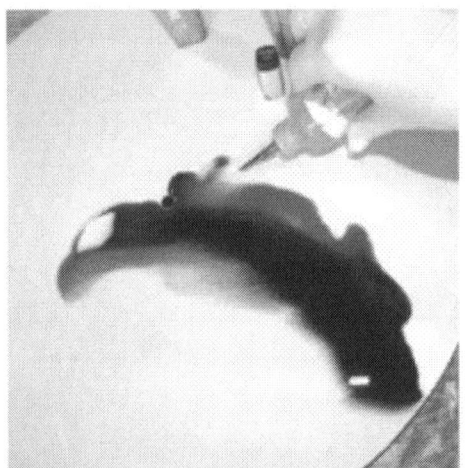

With the hairdryer on the first speed, I start drying gently on one side, then the other. I try to dry the ink stain on the inside with a hairdryer and go in a circle, wrapping the pattern.

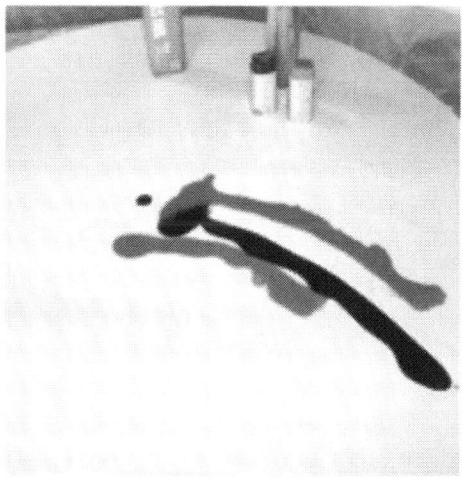

❖ The way you blow the hairdryer across the ink spot is how you'll form the pattern. If you move the hairdryer left and right in a straight motion, you won't have a curve, just a straight line. Or you can make a wave by moving the ink spot with the hairdryer in the shape of a wave.

❖ Remember, the hairdryer is your brush, and you set the pattern (direction) with your movements with the flow of air.

❖ Dry slowly, don't rush, and don't stop. Don't be spare alcohol on the outside of your work; otherwise, your ink will dry quickly and leave a hard edge between the successive waves, and there will be no beautiful lines at all.

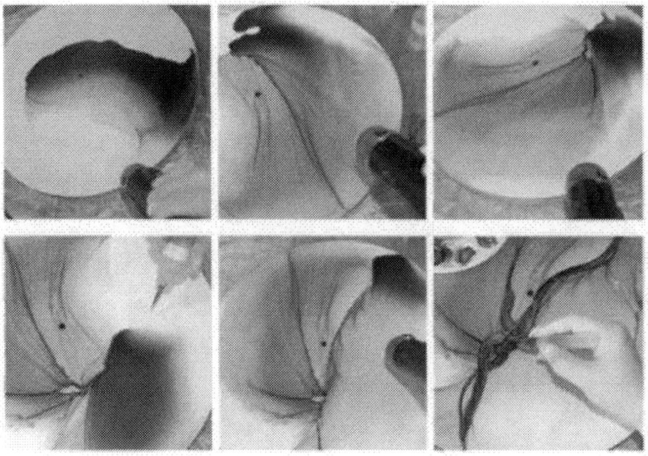

❖

You can add metallics to work or draw lines if you wish. Add ink and mix with alcohol to bring out your color if necessary. And so go around in a circle. Get to where you started.

The second version of applying ink in a circle

I apply two colors of ink - Copic "Blue" B97 and Pinata "Purpure" - to one part of the circle. I add alcohol to the ink so that it opens up. I add metallics and then add alcohol again.

I move the ink spot from right to left with the airflow in a smooth, slow motion. I move the ink spot to the center a little. Nice edges appear due to the metallics. The goal is to constantly move the ink spot to the center and go in a circle.

I move the air stream near the ink spot without touching the edge. This means that the hairdryer should be about 3 cm away from the edge of the ink when I drive it.

I move the ink spot with airflow, creating a winding line, thus creating an exciting drawing. If necessary, I add ink with alcohol and use a brush with a silicone tip to help the ink move in the direction I want.

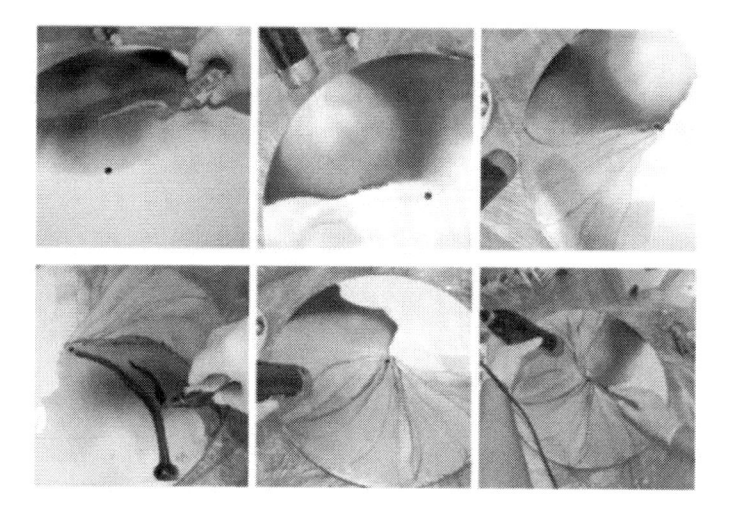

When I finish drying, I have a lot of ink left, so I collect it with a paper towel. I blot the ink with the napkin without stopping the drying process and finish the drawing. I do this at the very end to avoid damaging the pattern.

To have a finished composition, you can add fancy lines to the drawing with a brush, ink, and alcohol. I added lines exactly where the edges were torn.

Lesson 20: Petry

The artist Josie Lewis launched a new direction in art called Petrified Rainbow. She added alcohol ink to epoxy resin and got terrific shapes in a petri dish resembling coral reefs.

To get such "coral reefs," **you will need:**

- Silicone mold with a smooth surface (any - round, square, in the form of letters, etc.). It can also be purchased in a pastry store).

- Alcohol-based inks (Ranger "Mixative" or Penata "White" series pigments are required).

- Medium viscosity epoxy resin for creativity (100 g).

- Alcohol.

- Plastic little cups.
- Wooden spatula.
- Burner.
- Gloves.
- The mask is a respirator.
- Apron.
- Polyethylene film.

❖ *Always take precautions when working with epoxy: work in a well-ventilated room, without children or animals, and wear a mask, gloves, and apron.*

How I do it. Example:

I wipe the silicone mold with transparent scotch tape to remove debris and dust. I have a silicone mold in the shape of the letters "LOVE."

I mix the epoxy in the proportions given in the instructions (component A and component B).

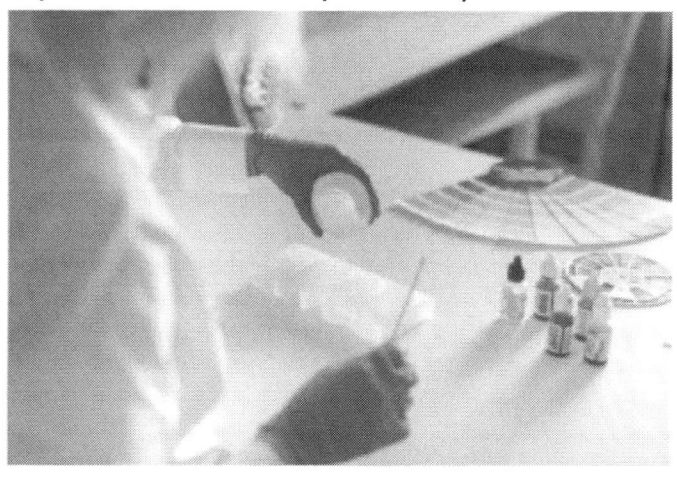

I thoroughly mix the resin and hardener with a wooden spatula for 4-5 minutes - not quickly, scraping off the walls of the glass. After mixing, the mixture should be as transparent as water. The formation of bubbles in the resin is normal.

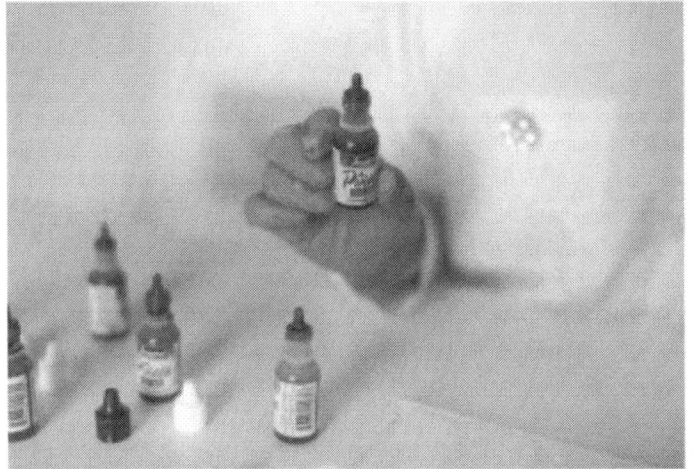

I pour the entire epoxy mixture into the mold. If bubbles form, I remove them with a gas torch, but the torch must be used quickly, without stopping in one place; otherwise, the resin will turn yellow.

After that, wait 20 minutes for the resin to solidify to medium viscosity. I take Pinata inks in different colors. They are very bright and are well suited for this Petry effect.

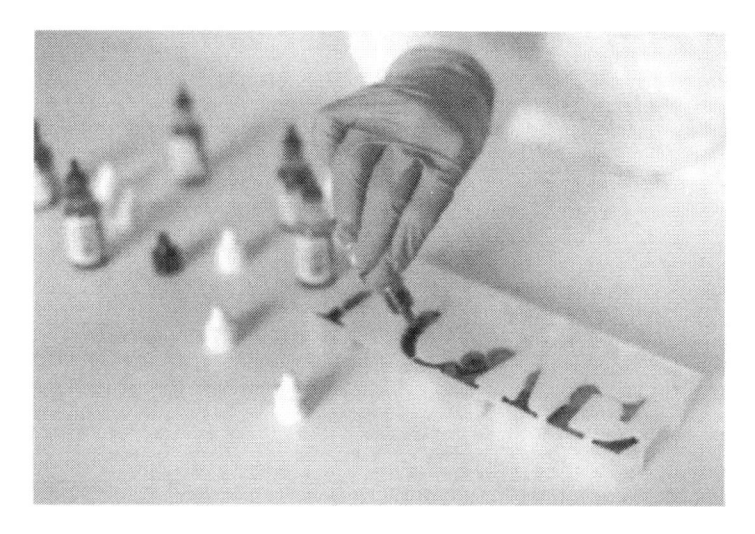

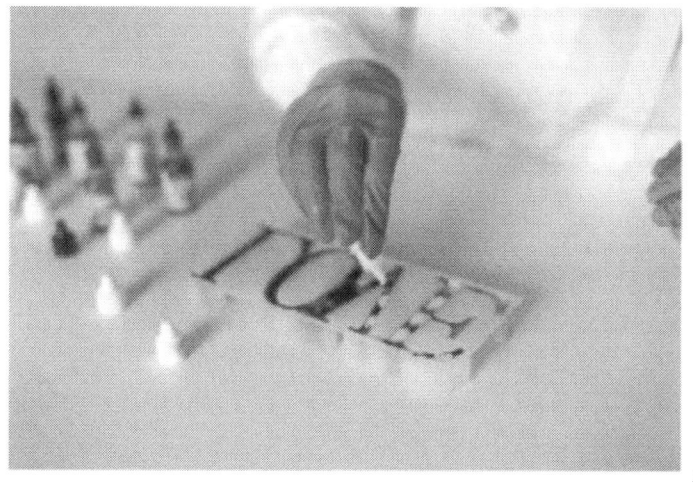

After 20-25 minutes, I drop the first layer of 1 drop of ink (blue) in the resin on all the letters. After, I add one drop of ink (magenta) with the second color. Then on top of the first layer of colors, I carefully add one drop of white color Penata or Mixative.

The drop should disperse very slowly. Observe. With white pigment, the drop curls, and the magic begins to happen.

Then I alternate pigments, following the sequence: a drop of color a drop of white Mixative; a drop of color - white Mixative. I do a maximum of 4 such layers.

❖ *The white Mixative or Penata sinks the ink to the bottom, creating magical patterns. If you add more and more color on top, it will penetrate the resin under the pressure of the weight of the new drops.*

After a while, as the ink penetrates the resin (the magic of ink curdling will pass after 5-7 minutes), you can carefully make a spiral inside the mold with a toothpick or a needle.

By swirling the resin and ink, I create a beautiful swirl that can only be seen the next day after the resin has cured. I work carefully with the needle to avoid scratching the bottom of the mold. I take the needle out carefully, removing the excess resin so that the pattern does not change. You can make different shapes with the needle in the form of zigzag lines and vertical lines in the form of feathers and curls.

I cover the mold with cardboard or a box to protect it from dust and leave it until the resin is fully cured. As a rule, you have to keep it for 24 hours.

Extract the resulting word from the form, starting from the sides.

❖ If you drip and the paint circles too quickly, the resin will still be too liquid; you need to wait a little longer. The droplet should spread out very slowly.

❖ If you use a very thick resin, the dye (ink) will not penetrate, and in a very liquid resin, the dye will fall to the bottom. A solid white color will form on the bottom of the mold, as I did on the letter "V" (in the middle of the letter is a solid white spot).

❖ With this technique, you can create entire worlds: paintings, tables, coasters, plates, caskets, beads, costume jewelry, etc.

❖ If you like resin products, you can read more about the technique in my first book, The Resin Guide.

Lesson 21: Masking Fluid and Clear Silhouette

You can create original drawings using masking fluid. It can have the most unexpected effects.

Masking liquid is liquid latex. The liquid has different colors (blue, yellow, turquoise). Applying this liquid to any ink surface allows you to protect areas of your work from being accidentally painted over.

Brands that make Masking Fluid include Pebeo Liquid Latex Masking Fluid Drawing Gum, Schmincke, Sennelier, Winsor & Newton, MOLOTOW, etc.

Silhouettes in alcohol ink and masking fluid

You will need: synthetic paper, a printed silhouette or whatever you want, a cutter, backing (what to cut the drawing on), alcohol ink (Pinata Pink, Ranger "Slate", Ranger "Aqua", Liquid chrome), alcohol, masking fluid, thin synthetic brush, gloves, mask.

How I do it. Example:

I cut out a silhouette outline with a paper knife. I outline the person's silhouette(s) on the synthetic paper with a simple pencil.

❖

To make the pencil less visible, you can wipe the clear outlines lightly with a rag soaked in alcohol. I don't recommend erasing the pencil with an eraser, as it leaves unsightly stains on the synthetic paper.

Next, I use masking fluid to create an outline beyond which the ink will not protrude. I apply the masking fluid outside of the outline. The painted part will be in the center of the silhouette.

I wait for the latex to dry for about 5 to 10 minutes - the masking liquid should dry during this time (you will see it covered with a thin film).

❖ *Brushes with natural fleece can be ruined. It is recommended to apply the fluid with a synthetic brush. Rinse brushes immediately after application. Please do not keep the fluid for several days without removing it from the pattern; it may not come off the surface well, as its properties change over time.*

Then I put ink all over the inside surface. My drawing is a silhouette of a man and a woman. I put drops of Pinata "Pink" and Ranger "Slate" on the drawing on the woman's side. I also added silver in a random pattern.

I drop in Ranger "Aqua" and Ranger "Slate" on the male side and randomly add Molotow ink (silver).

I add alcohol and start blowing with a hairdryer on the first speed in a circle to get beautiful streaks.

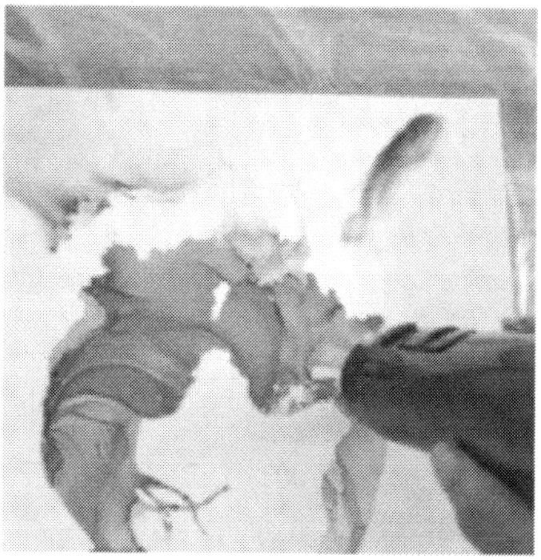

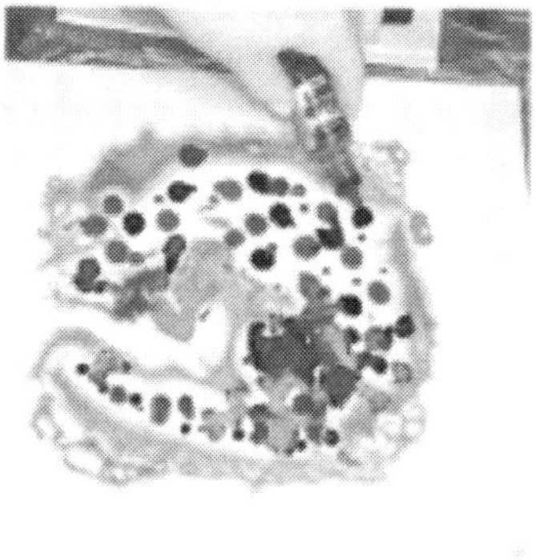
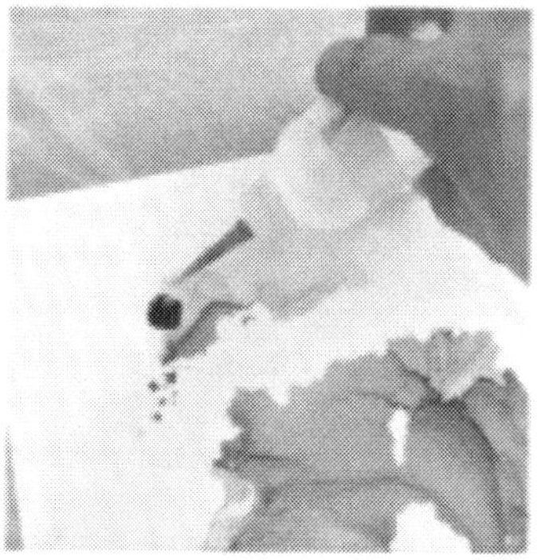
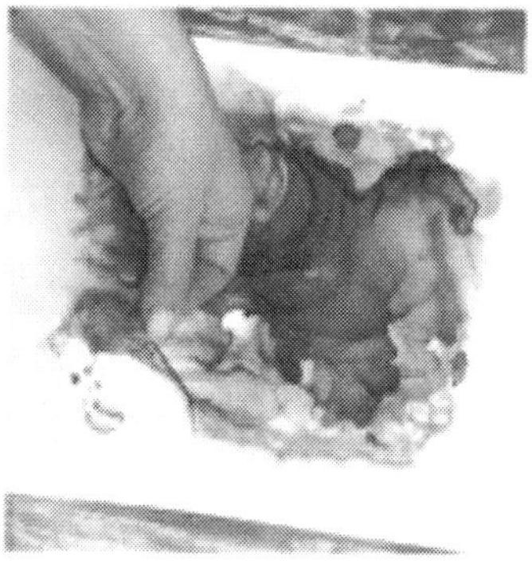

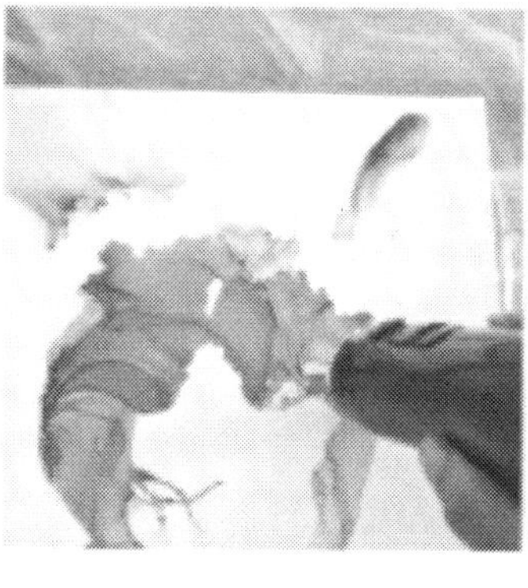
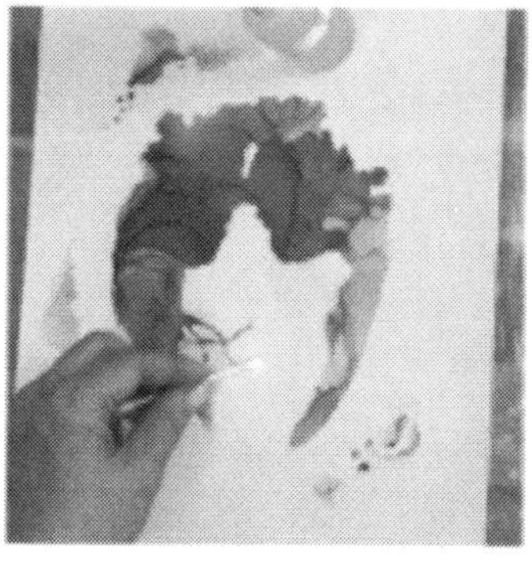
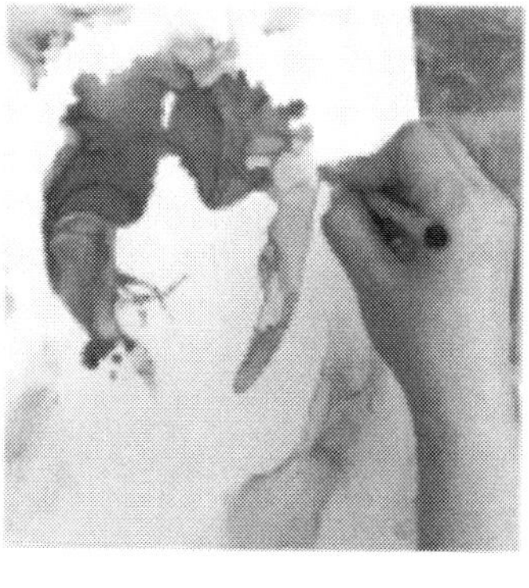

❖ *If you have a large drawing, apply the ink in small portions to the surface and dry it in a circular blowing pattern before applying the next portion of the ink.*

When the job has been completed and the ink is completely dry, I gently remove the dried masking film (latex fluid) with my fingers. I remove the film as if rolling it over the surface.

❖ *This is the most fun part. Did you enjoy removing the film? Share your feedback about it, please.*

With alcohol and an ear stick, I remove the sweat and the extra elements formed during the work.

Using a black marker, I trace the outline of the silhouettes to emphasize the expressiveness of the drawing. You can finish the drawing at this stage if you think the composition is finished. You can frame it. But I wanted to add some lightness on all sides of the silhouettes and get away from the precise boundaries.

With the help of alcohol and a hairdryer, I slightly blur the bottom contours and dry them. You can also use a brush - fan to create a drip effect.

❖ *Frame your creative work in a frame with a mat. This will make it stand out and give it a distinctive look. Use the masking fluid to create silhouettes of animals, people, and insects that will blend beautifully into your interior.*

Lesson 22: Drawing on Glass and Ceramics with Ink

The decorating technique on ceramics and glass is enjoyed by adults and children alike. Even the simplest white mug can add juicy bright accents with ink.

The pattern will be light and airy on the transparent glass but will be pronounced on ceramics.

What you need for this:
- Cover your work surface with foil,
- Prepare several colors of alcohol ink (Pinata / Copic / Ranger's),
- Prepare metallic ink, isopropyl alcohol,
- Any form, gloves, mask,
- The tassel is a fan; the brush is thin,
- Food or wrapping film,
- Acrylic glue (sprayer) or for decoupage on glass and ceramics.

How I do it. Example:

The first option is to apply the ink:

At the beginning of the work, I degrease the ceramic surface of the flowerpot with alcohol using a paper towel. The back of the vase can be protected with molar tape, but I did not do so this time.

I put drops of alcohol ink of different colors on the clingfilm in a chaotic pattern. Then I place the flower pot on the clingfilm and press it to the clingfilm.

I squeeze the film with my hands so that gatherings and folds form. I leave it like that for a couple of hours.

❖ *Don't straighten the film!*

After the ink has dried, I carefully remove the film - the ceramic surface has a fun pattern.

I fix the drawing with protective acrylic varnish or varnish for decoupage. I apply the varnish in two to three layers with intervals between 30 minutes and then wait until the varnish dries completely (a couple of hours).

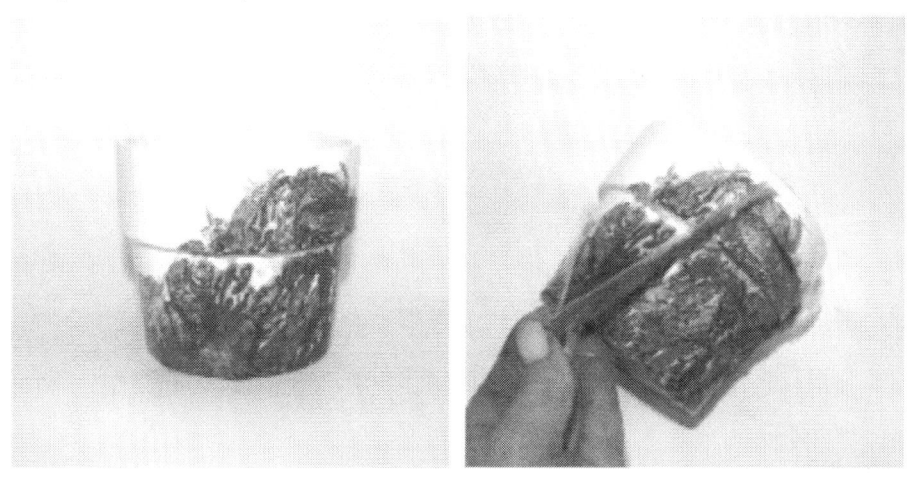

The second option is to apply the ink:

I put a paper napkin on a table covered with foil to absorb the ink.

I tape the top edge of the ceramic mug with painter's tape, turn it upside down and place it on the napkin.

I apply different ink colors to the entire ceramic surface from the top of the mug's base in a circular pattern.

Then I pour alcohol from a bottle over this ink. I do this several times until I get the effect I want.

The ink and alcohol create beautiful streaks all over the mug's surface.
I let the ink drain down well and dry.

I wipe off any excess drips on the bottom of the mug with alcohol using a napkin or sponge. I then turn the mug upside down.
I fix the drawing with protective acrylic varnish or decoupage varnish. I apply the varnish in two to three layers with a break of 30 minutes.

I wait for the varnish to dry completely (a couple of hours) and then wash the mug from the inside with a soapy solution.

Everything! So the mug is safe for use.

The third option is to apply the ink:

First, I degrease the surface of the white ceramic bowl with a paper towel moistened with alcohol.

Then I use a fan brush to apply ink of one color and distribute this ink on the bowl's surface. You can apply it both horizontally and vertically.

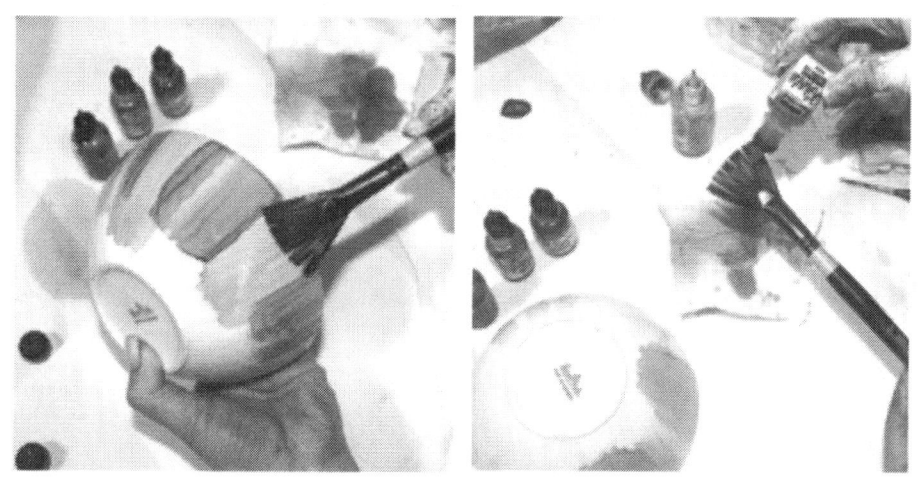

Next, I use the same fan brush to apply alcohol and ink in different colors. I do this all over the surface of the bowl. I get beautiful blurry stripes on the surface.

❖ *You can experiment with layering the ink and bring it to your desired effect.*

❖ Over horizontal lines, I make dots with a brush soaked in alcohol. You can create any pattern you want.

I fix the picture with protective acrylic varnish or decoupage varnish. After the varnish dries completely, you can use the bowl.

The fourth option is to apply the ink:

On a degreased ceramic surface, you can create any kind of subject drawings with alcohol ink, a brush, and alcohol. Nail design brushes are ideal for drawing small details. This technique is somewhat similar to watercolor.

❖ *If I need to lighten an area, I add a little alcohol. You can use a palette with several colors on it to help.*

I fix the pattern with protective acrylic varnish or decoupage varnish. After the varnish dries completely, you can use the product.

❖ Spray the lacquer in a well-ventilated room at a distance of 30 cm from the product. Coat with a thin layer so that the lacquer does not drip on the product. Wait for the varnish to dry (up to 30 minutes), and then apply the varnish again in a thin layer.

❖ After 24 hours, your product is safe to use; wash it with your hands. It is not recommended to wash such items in the dishwasher or with abrasive sponges; otherwise, your pattern will be erased.

With these simple techniques, you can decorate anything: vases, Christmas toys, mugs, flower pots, lamps for the house, coasters, teapots, dishes for eating on the outside, plafonds, and other decorative items. You can add crystals to the design with glue or use a dotting technique with a ceramic marker.

Lesson 23: Black Surfaces

White, pearlescent, nude inks, and metallics like gold, silver, and bronze are mainly used on black surfaces. I think acid colors will also look attractive on dark surfaces.

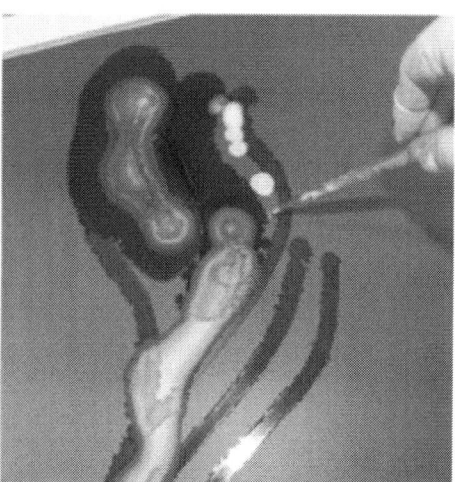

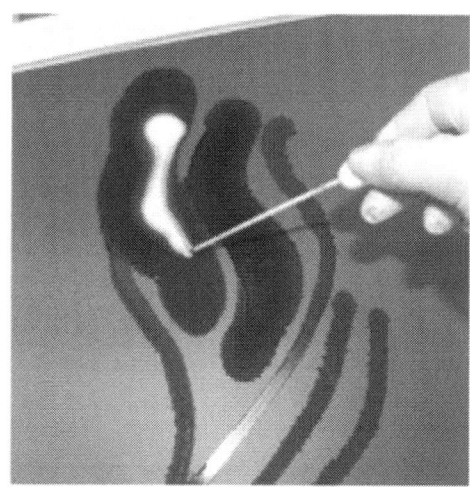

Pictures with a dark surface of large size look more effective. I have a square of 50*50 cm.

White is the lightest, most contrasting color. The main thing is to not overdo with its quantity. stir Stir white pigment from Ranger

"Mexative" or Pinata "White" in a cup with alcohol; because it is very thick, it will settle on the surface of the spots.

How I do it. Example:

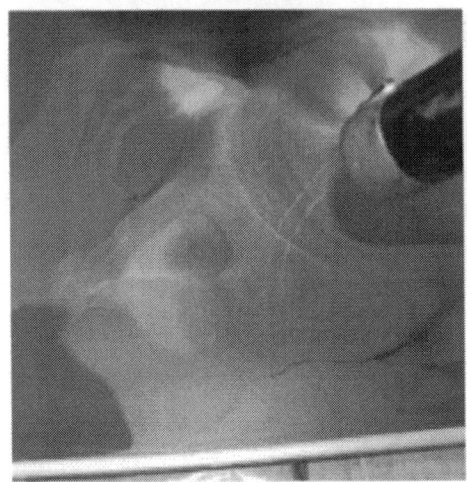

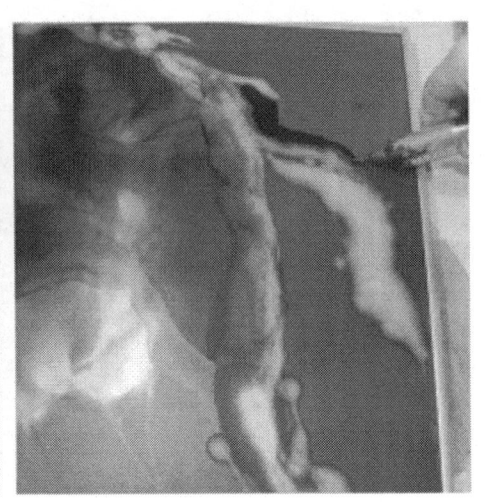

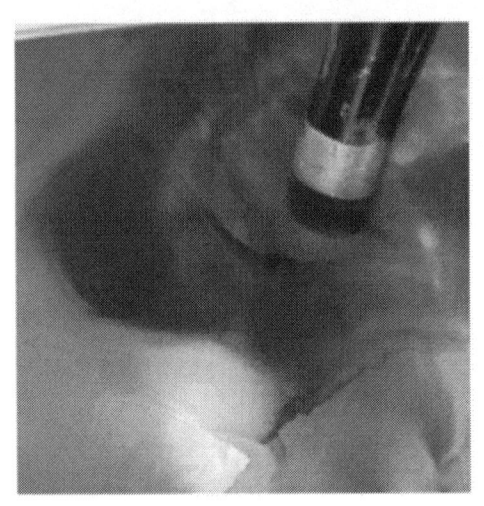

I apply the ink in a chaotic pattern on a dark ink surface. I have Ranger "Rasberry," Ranger "Stonewashed," Pinata "Rich Gold," and Ranger "Mexative" white pigment.

I place the colored ink next to the white ink - a short distance from the white spot. These colors will not mix with the white, and the drawing will look airier when drying.

❖   *When adding metallics (gold, silver, bronze), it is necessary to run a finger over the surface so as not to form a solid stain.*

I add a large amount of isopropyl alcohol and slowly start drying the work, skirting the stain, creating a composition.

❖   *Try not to correct the work in the process because the white color dissolves very poorly when you add the alcohol again.*

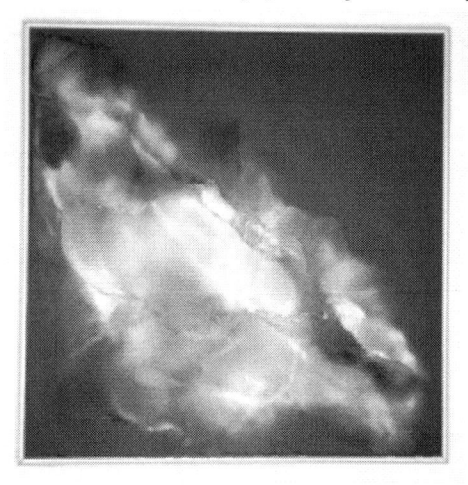

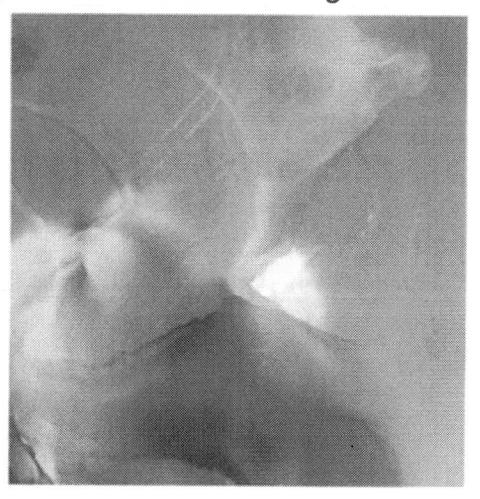

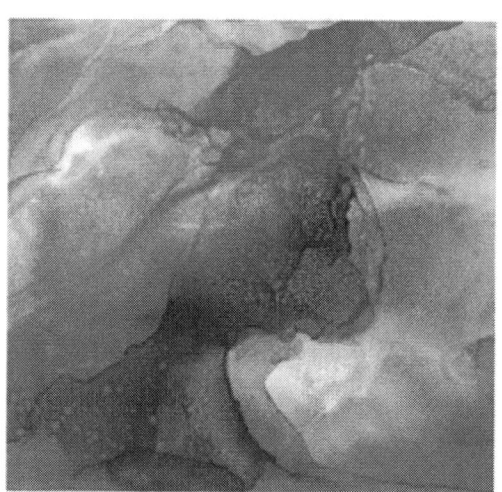

After drying one part, I move on to the other, introducing colors. At the end of the work, I apply a "splash" effect to make the work easier.

Lesson 24: Collages (mini-pictures)

Coloring paper is a preparatory and exciting process where you can include imagination. Collages are created on wooden surfaces from pieces of pre-inked synthetic paper (100-150 microns). Then individual elements are cut out of the colored paper and glued to the wooden surface.

Collage is a mixed technique. Such paintings are covered at the end with a transparent layer of epoxy resin on top.

You can dye synthetic paper in many different ways:

- Pour the ink onto the paper and smear it with a dab hand.
- Pour the ink in different colors and put a transparent film on top, wrinkle it, and leave it to dry completely. After removing the film, you will get unusual and beautiful stains.

- Pour the ink in different colors, put the transparent film on top, leave it until it is scorched, and then remove it.

   - Pour ink of different colors and distribute it by tilting the paper in different directions.
   - Pour ink of different colors and distribute with a brush - a fan of color on the paper.
   - You can also use spray-on wet or dried ink.

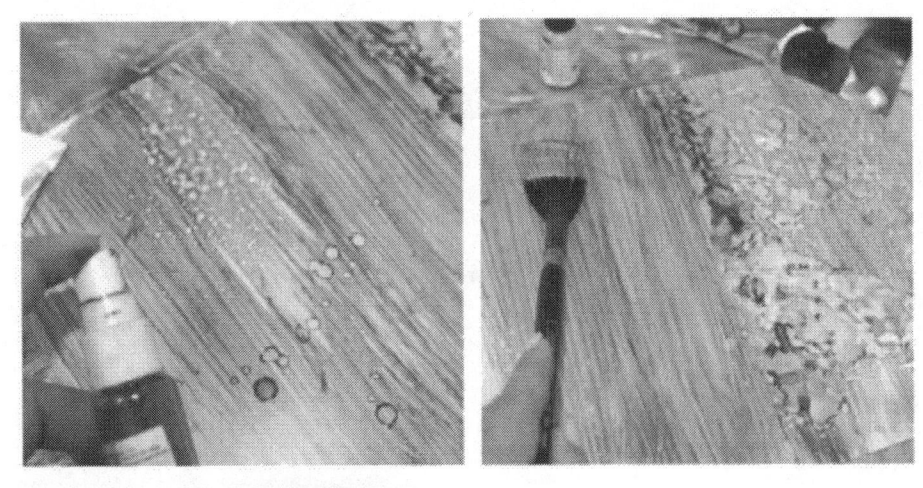

- Pour ink in different colors and dry either with a hairdryer or leave it to dry on its own.

Take two small pieces of synthetic paper. On one of them, apply alcohol ink in a chaotic pattern, cover the top with a piece of paper, then gently separate from each other.

How I do it. Example:

I glue the synthetic paper onto the wooden base. I use Tesa or Golden spray glue. They don't cause any yellow stains. After it dries, I cut off the excess paper. The next step is to cut out the elements of the paper for the picture according to the idea.

I distribute the cutout elements on the surface. I glue these cutout elements to the wooden base. I glue each element carefully so that there are no bubbles. I use pens or markers to trace the details of the entire drawing.

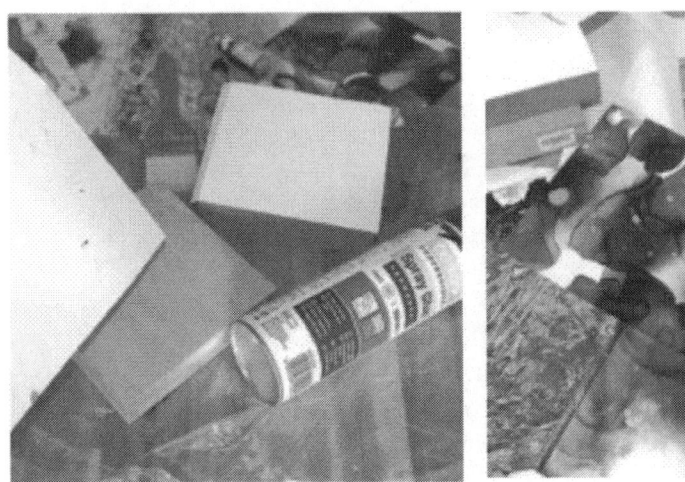

I coat the entire work with protective and UV varnish. I wait until the work is arid.

❖   *Varnish protection is necessary before coating with resin; otherwise, the colors under the epoxy may change or disappear partially.*

I coat the work with a transparent layer of epoxy, forming a lens.

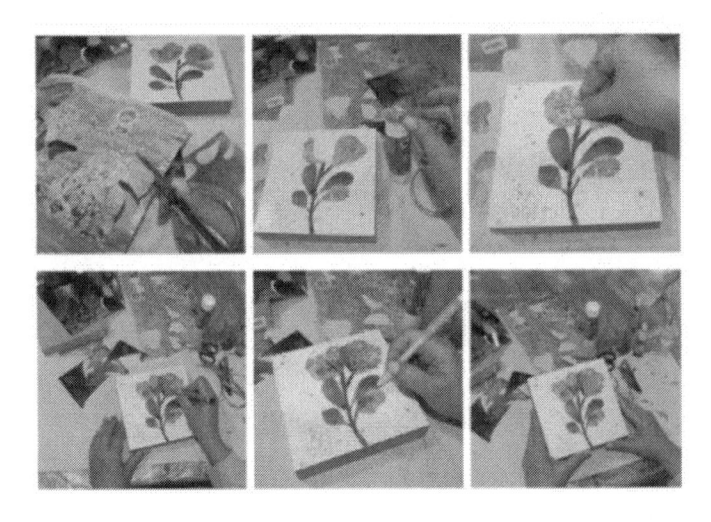

❖ *Apply safety precautions when working with resin (respirator, gloves, open window). You can read more about epoxy resin in my book "The Resin Guide." (Reference in Chapter 9)*

Try, experiment, and enjoy what you get, because the ink can surprise you!

18. THE APPLICATION OF PAINTING WITH ALCOHOL INK

The range of applications of the technology described above is extensive. Here is a list of options, where else (except for the cases mentioned above) you can apply for decorative work with alcohol ink (ideas for reflection).

1. Wall decorations. Paintings with cut-out figures

On synthetic paper, distribute the ink randomly over the entire surface. Fix it with varnish, and wait for it to dry. Next, cut out any shapes from the paper (butterflies, letters, hearts) and use double-sided tape to model the walls.

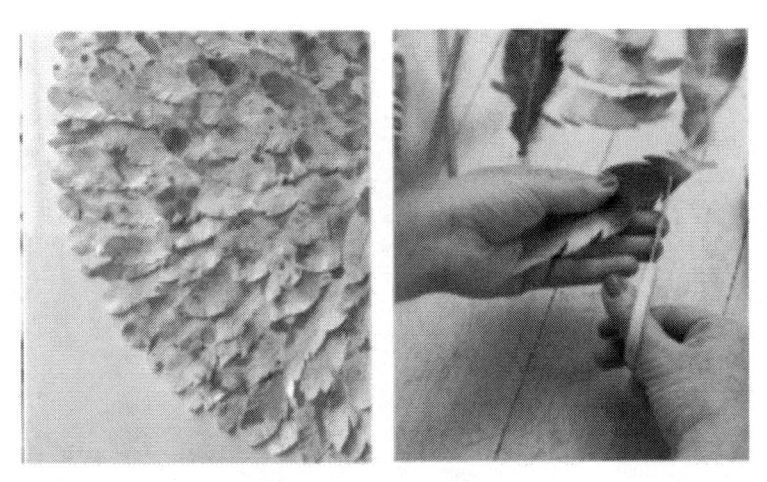

These are paintings by two sisters - Claire Scholes and Joy Stewart. They gave me the idea that such wall panels could be created using alcoholic painting.

2. Interior printing on high-density seamless fabrics

Modern technology allows us to preserve our creativity by transferring the picture to the wallpaper. This can be ordered from any creative printing company. A great idea to make one wall in any room an accent wall. Wallpapers with delicate colors and those with more air in the picture will look more interesting. The picture is applied with modern environmentally-friendly latex paints, which are waterproof and do not burn out—great decor for the whole wall.

3. Decorating the "apron" in the kitchen

You can make an original accent on your kitchen with such a design. One nuance: the "apron" decoration will look more advantageous if your kitchen set is in monochrome colors.

An exciting variant of painting for such a decoration is an imitation of marble or the usual airy, abstract motifs.

Lay out the tiles or glass on the table and ink the entire surface so that the pattern looks uniform. Do not forget to fix with acrylic and ultraviolet varnish in three to four layers. Choose for work tiles with a smooth, glossy, not rough texture. You can also decorate glass coasters in the form of tiles in the tone of the "apron."

Another option is to print your picture on white tiles for the kitchen "apron."

I had a children's bathroom print with pictures of the kids. Unfortunately, I can't show you, but it looks imposing! You give the scanning element of your picture, painted in alcohol ink, to the printmaker.

4. Stationery of all kinds

Bookmarks for books, envelopes, postcards, the insert for the purchase of "Thank you," a transparent phone case, etc. can all be decorated with a painting made of alcohol ink.

5. Paintings created with Paper Cutting Art

How can you spectacularly decorate the walls in a child's room or hallway? I cut out any pattern or silhouette from a single-colored thick paper with a silhouette cutter. For example, from two colors - colored and white paper.

Separately, I make a backing on synthetic paper. I put alcohol ink on the paper and create any fancy drawing. Instead of top-heavy paper, you can make any pattern out of synthetic paper and then cut out any pattern with a knife.

Then we put the layers on top of each other and fixed everything with double-sided tape. We used frames from IKEA and ended up with these cute mini-pictures.

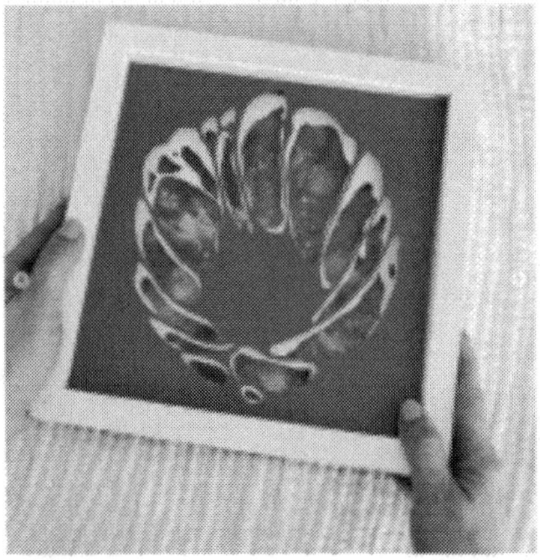
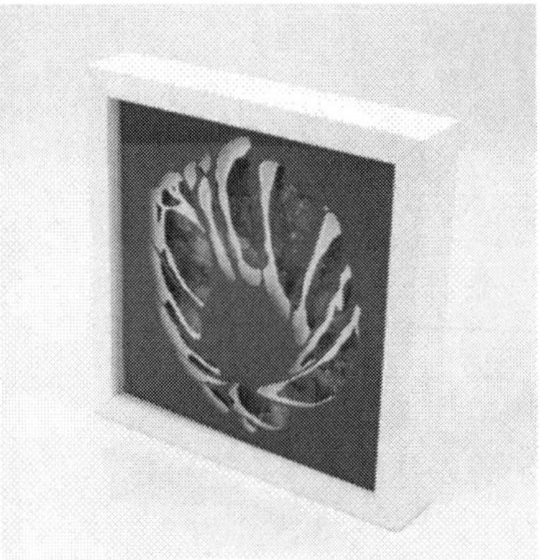

19. DESIGN AND VIZUALIZATION OF PAINTINGS

How can you decorate your work to make it look complete? The choice on the market is enormous. Either you choose baguette shops, art stores, or interior design stores.

The following options are available for picture design:

- We decorate in baguettes—aluminum baguettes in different color variations (gold, silver, brass).
- It is framed with protective plastic—Interior stores, like IKEA.
- Under Glass. Make sure the painting is arid before framing it under glass.
- On a wood base. Glue synthetic paper to a rigid base, and then you can frame it or leave it that way.
- On a wide stretcher, the picture does not need to be decorated.
- Paintings framed in a frame with a mat are beautiful to look at. Frames can be round, oval, square, or rectangular.

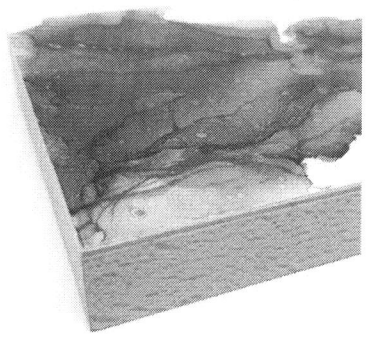

20. BEGINNER'S CHCKLIST

The practice of decorative painting with alcohol ink will require many materials, tools, and supplies.

- ❖ I recommend that you don't buy an entire palette of alcohol ink at once. Choose 3 to 4 colors.
- ❖ I also advise you to buy a small volume of isopropyl alcohol to start with.
- ❖ Take a disposable 3M respirator.
- ❖ You can do without UV varnish at the beginning of your studies when you try this technique.
- ❖ When you realize that you are strongly attracted to this technique and want more, buy all the missing materials.

A brief checklist of materials and tools needed for the beginner is shown in the table below.

N	Product name	Notes
1	Alcohol ink or alcohol refills for markers	Copic, Piñata, Ranger /Adirondack /Tim Holtz, Huids, Touch, Pentart.
2	Isopropyl Absolute Alcohol or Blending Solution.	99.7 – 99.9%.
3	The basis for painting - any laminated surface	Synthetic paper or paper for banners 250; 300; 450 microns; Artboards with laminated surface.
4	Hairdryer - comb with low power (travel)	Power from 600 to 1000 W
5	Dense film to protect the work surface	At any construction store
6	Transparent bottle with pointed spout for alcohol	In the art store.
7	Paper napkins, vinyl or nitrile gloves	Sold in supermarkets and hardware stores.
8	Brush, ear wands, water brush, rubber blower, spray bottle	To create additional effects
9	UV protective varnish for works and fixing varnish.	Pebeo Vernis A Tableau Mat; Krylon's Kamar® Varnish. UV Protectant; Golden; Montana Gold
10	Respirator for respiratory protection	3M mask with charcoal filters

Made in the USA
Columbia, SC
06 February 2024